Ohio Valley Historical Series.

NUMBER THREE.

———

CLARK'S

Campaign in the Illinois.

Engraved by T. H. Welch from a Portrait by J.B. Longacre after an original painting by J. W. Jarvis.

GEORGE ROGERS CLARK.

Col. George Rogers Clark's

SKETCH OF HIS

Campaign in the Illinois

in 1778-9

WITH

AN INTRODUCTION

By Hon. Henry Pirtle, of Louisville

AND

AN APPENDIX

CONTAINING

The Public and Private Instructions to Col. Clark

AND

MAJOR BOWMAN'S JOURNAL

OF THE

Taking of Post St. Vincents.

PUBLISHED IN COOPERATION WITH
HISTORIC LOCUST GROVE, INC.
LOUISVILLE, KENTUCKY

APPLEWOOD BOOKS
Bedford, Massachusetts

Clark's Campaign in the Illinois was first published in 1869
by Robert Clarke & CO. of Cincinnati.

Thank you for purchasing an Applewood Book.
Applewood reprints America's lively classics—
books from the past that are still of interest
to modern readers. For a free copy of our
current catalog, write to:
Applewood Books
P.O. Box 365
Bedford, MA 01730

ISBN 1-55709-584-1

Library of Congress Control Number: 2001012345

PUBLISHERS' NOTICE.

THE letter here printed for the first time, was presented to the Historical Society of Kentucky by Hon. George Mason, of Gunston Hall, Virginia, to whom it was addressed. We are indebted to Hon. Henry Pirtle, of Louisville, for the privilege of incorporating it in our SERIES, and also for the Introduction.

We have endeavored to follow the manuscript as closely as was possible in print, adding only a word here and there (in italics), which seemed necessary to complete the sense. To have modernized it would have required so many alterations, that we thought it unadvisable to make the attempt. A few notes have been added which may be of some use or interest to the reader.

We have appended the "public" and "private"

instructions received by Col. Clark, for his guidance during the expedition, from Patrick Henry, Governor of Virginia, and also the "Journal" kept by Major Bowman during a portion of the campaign—the taking of Post St. Vincents—and revised by some unknown "person who was in the expedition." The manuscript of this Journal was at one·time in the possession of the Historical Society of Kentucky, but has unfortunately been lost.

CONTENTS.

(vii)

Introductory.

ALL GENERATIONS of American people will owe a debt, that can not be measured, to the memory of Colonel GEORGE ROGERS CLARK, and his brave officers and soldiers, for the results of the campaign the progress of which is so simply narrated in the ensuing pages. This is the original letter sent by Colonel—afterward General—Clark, to the illustrious revolutionary statesman, George Mason, of Virginia, his friend and patron.

On the second[1] of January, seventeen hundred and eighty-one, the Legislature of Virginia declared in certain resolutions passed that day, that "Colonel George Rogers Clark planned and executed the secret expedition by which the British posts between the Ohio and Mississippi rivers were reduced." In this undertaking he had not even the advice of General Washington, or of any other officer, and was at the time only twenty-five years of age. But for this conquest made by Colonel Clark for the United States—

and particularly for Virginia—in the midst of the‾ terrible struggle with England, the boundary of our land, conquered in the revolution from Great Britain, would, in all probability, have been the eastern bank of the Ohio, or the Allegheny mountains, instead of the eastern shore of the Mississippi.*

This whole country between the rivers, in no very definite expressions, had been transferred by France to England by the treaty of Paris, 1763, and possession rather indefinitely delivered in 1765. The people of Illinois, in 1771, demanded a government of their own by the people, as free and bold as had been claimed as an English and American principle in New England and South Carolina ; and in 1772

---

* The following letter of Mr. Jefferson shows his anticipation of the importance of this expedition :

                          " *Williamsb*†   *   *   *

Col. Geo. R. Clark,
        Sir :
               Your letter and verba   *   *   * by Mr. St. Vrain was received to-day. Your w   *   *   * attended to. Much solicitude will be felt for the result of your expedition to the Wabash ; it will, at least, delay their expedition to the frontier settlement, and if successful, have an important bearing ultimately in establishing our northwestern boundary.
          I am, sir, your most obedient,
                    TH. JEFFERSON."

---

† A portion of the letter has been torn off and lost.

they sent through their agent in London, Daniel Blinn, their indignant protest to Lord Dartmouth, the British Secretary, against a new government proposing to put them under the officers of the crown only. This government against which they protested, included Vincennes, which had then been settled more than seventy years. These facts are alluded to as showing the direct and sole possession and acknowledged dominion of Great Britain at the time of our revolution.

Yet Spain and France both contended in the preliminary negotiations at Paris in 1782, that this great land could not be ceded to the United States, that they had no legal claim to it. Dr. Franklin, in August, this year, when engaged in these negotiations at Paris, speaking of the claim of Spain to the western country, says: " My conjecture of that court's design to coop us up within the Allegheny mountains, is now manifest. I hope Congress will insist on the Mississippi as the boundary, and the free navigation of the river from which they would exclude us."

The claim that Spain made was futile, and could not bear examination. She could not connect her claim to the Lower Mississippi with this territory. The constructive possession could not reach up so far; Clark had built Fort Jefferson below the mouth of the Ohio, and Virginia had actual possession also between the rivers. This was the pretense of Spain; in the winter of 1781, a detachment of about sixty-five Spaniards, accompanied by about the same number of Indians, took possession of a small English Fort, called St. Joseph, situated near the source of the Illinois river. They hoisted the Spanish standard, and pretended to take possession of the fort, and its dependencies, and of the river Illinois, in the name of the Spanish king. This was what the Spanish minister called a conquest: and he insisted that, if the country did not belong to the king of Spain, it did not belong to the Americans, but to the Indians.

France could make no claim: she could only dispute the claim of the colonies, or of the United States; and even this she forebore to do through her principal minister the Count de Vergennes, but Rayneval, the principal secretary of the great minister, was put forward, to make this dispute.

The negotiations at Paris in 1782, as far especially as Spain and France were concerned, were for the matters of compromises between these powers respectively and Great Britain; and they so ended as far as these three powers were concerned; and it did not matter to them how the Americans came. out in these negotiations. The object in regard to the western country, was to keep it out of the hands of the United States, and then it could be set off to one or other of the three powers in consideration of something else. England was then temporizing with Spain, as the issues of these conferences between England, Spain, and France showed to every observer. How else could Spain have claimed anything in the face of Britain? But the

English envoy could not pretend that it did not belong
to the colonies that had set themselves up as the United
States. The conquest had been fully made by Clark in
1778 and 1779; and in October, 1778, the county of Illinois was established by the General Assembly of Virginia,
covering all the territory, and provision was made for its protection by reinforcements to the army of Clark; and in
May, 1780, the act of October, 1778, was continued and
amended, and other reinforcements ordered by Virginia.
In fact, as an almost natural result from Clark's campaign,
the land between the rivers was actually under the government *de facto*, as well as *de jure*, of this country, for
it could not be denied that the patent of Virginia, with
some portion to other colonies, covered the whole region,
so that the arms of Clark had settled the question of
possession, and civil, as well as military rule, of this great
territory, which now holds so many millions of people.
These prominent facts were before the British minister,
and before the world. He could not say, then, that this
part of the land was in the power of England, any more than
Virginia herself was after the battle of Yorktown; and he
was too accurate a jurist to yield to any claim of Spain,
or to hear the objections of France. But what would
have been the judgment of Great Britain, beset by France
and Spain, and looking to its own aggrandizement, as every
country does, if this campaign had never been made? The
force of conquest, the moving etiquette of treaties of peace,
would have been lost.

But there are additional facts springing out of this conquest. The act of Congress of 1780 recommended to the several states to cede their out-lands, such as those west of the Ohio, to Congress, looking, of course, to what had been done by Clark. And the act of Virginia of October 20, 1783, about the transfer of these lands to Congress, recites the act of Congress of 1780 and the Virginia act of 1781, concerning these same lands. And Virginia, on 2d January, 1781, granted one hundred and fifty thousand acres to the officers and soldiers of Clark, and the same act reserved land for other officers and soldiers between the rivers Scioto and Little Miami.

Now, the preliminary articles of peace and boundary had been under negotiation for months, and were signed by Oswald for England, and by Adams, Franklin, Jay, and Laurens for America, on the 30th of November, 1782, when, of course, these things had been well understood; and afterward, on the 3d of September, 1783, the definite treaty of peace and boundary was signed at Paris by Hartley for England, and Adams, Franklin, and Jay for the United States. Surely all that had followed the campaign of Colonel Clark, had been well debated and considered, and but for our holding the country under military and civil rule, as much a part of the United States as any other portion of its territory, we would have had our boundary, not the east bank of the Mississippi, but the east bank of the Ohio, or the ridge of the ˙Alleghenies. In contemplating the depth of our gratitude, let us think whether New

Orleans and St. Louis and all the great country of Louisiana would, in any reasonable probability, have been purchased of the First Consul, and come to us through Mr. Jefferson but for this campaign of Clark. No, certainly not. This magnificent country, made of this and other purchases, now extending as one with us to the north Pacific, might to this hour have been broken from us at the mountain's summit or the river's shore.

H. P.

Biographical Sketch.

[*The following sketch of the Life of General Clark is given in Lewis Collins'* HISTORICAL SKETCHES OF KENTUCKY.]

GENERAL GEORGE ROGERS CLARK, whose name is deservedly celebrated in the early history of Kentucky, and conspicuously prominent in the conquest and settlement of the whole west, was born in the county of Albemarle, in the State of Virginia, November 19, 1752. Of his early years and education, but little is known. In his youth, he engaged in the business of land surveying, which appears to have presented to the enterprising young men of that day, a most congenial and attractive field for the exercise of their energies. It is worthy of remark, that many of the most opulent and influential families of Kentucky were founded by men engaged in this pursuit. How long Clark engaged in this vocation, is unknown. He commanded a company in Dunsmore's war, and was engaged in the only active operation of the right wing of the invading army against the Indians. At the close of this war, he was offered a commission in the English service, but, upon consultation with his friends, he was induced by the troubled aspect of the relations between the colonies and Great Britain, to decline the appointment.

In the spring of 1775, he came to Kentucky, drawn hither by that love of adventure which distinguished him through life. He remained in Kentucky during the spring and summer of this year, familiarizing himself with the character of the people and the resources of the country, until the fall, when he returned to Virginia. During this visit, he was temporarily placed in command of the irregular militia of the settlements; but whether he held a commission is not known. In the spring of the following year (1776), he again came to Kentucky, with the intention of making it his permanent home; and from this time forth, his name is closely associated with the progress of the western settlements in power and civilization.

His mind had been very early impressed with the immense importance of this frontier country to the security of the parent State of Virginia, as well as to the whole confederacy; and his reflections on this subject led him to perceive the importance of a more thorough, organized, and extensive system of public defense, and a more regular plan of military operations, than the slender resources of the colonies had yet been able to effect. With the view of accomplishing this design, he had been in Kentucky but a few months, when he suggested to the settlers the propriety of convening a general assembly of the people at Harrodstown (now Harrodsburg), to take steps toward forming a more definite and certain connection with the government and people of Virginia than as yet existed. The immediate necessity for this movement grew out of the memorable and well known conflict between Henderson & Co. and the legislature of Virginia, relative to the disputed claim of jurisdiction over a large portion of the new territory. The excitement which arose out of this dispute, and the prevailing uncertainty whether the south side of Kentucky river appertained to Virginia or North Carolina (the latter claiming by virtue of Henderson's purchase of the Cherokees at the treaty of Wataga), added very greatly to the perplexity of the settlers, and rendered it necessary that the disposition of Virginia should be distinctly ascertained. The proposed meeting was accordingly held at Harrodstown on the 6th of June, 1776, at which Clark and Gabriel Jones were chosen members of the assembly of Virginia. This, however, was not precisely the thing contemplated by Clark. He wished that the people should appoint *agents*, with general powers to *negotiate* with the government of Virginia, and in the event that that commonwealth should refuse to recognize the colonists as within its jurisdiction and under its protection, he proposed to employ the lands of the country as a fund to obtain settlers and establish an independent State. The election had, however, gone too far to change its object when Clark arrived at Harrodstown, and the gentlemen elected, although aware that the choice could give them no seat in the legislature, proceeded to Williamsburg, at that time the seat of government. After suffering the most severe privations in their journey through the wilderness, the delegates found, on their arrival in Virginia, that the legislature had adjourned, whereupon Jones directed his steps to the settlements on Holston, and left Clark to attend to the Kentucky mission alone.

He immediately waited on Governor Henry, then lying sick at his residence in Hanover county, to whom he stated the objects of his journey. These meeting the approbation of the governor, he gave Clark a letter to the executive council of the State. With this letter in his hand he appeared before the council, and after acquainting them fully with the condition and circumstances of the colony, he made application for five hundred weight of gunpowder for the defense of the various stations. But with every disposition to assist and promote the growth of these remote and infant settlements, the council felt itself restrained by the uncertain and indefinite state of the relations existing between the colonists and the state of Virginia, from complying fully with his demand. The Kentuckians had not yet been recognized by the legislature as citizens, and the proprietary claimants, Henderson & Co., were at this time exerting themselves to obtain from Virginia a relinquishment of her jurisdiction of the new territory. The council, therefore, could only offer to *lend* the gunpowder to the colonists as *friends*, not *give* it to them as *fellow-citizens*. At the same time they required Clark to be personally responsible for its value, in the event the legislature should refuse to recognize the Kentuckians as citizens, and in the mean time to defray the expense of its conveyance to Kentucky. Upon these terms he did not feel at liberty to accept the proffered assistance. He represented to the council that the emissaries of the British were employing every means to engage the Indians in the war; that the people in the remote and exposed stations of Kentucky might be exterminated for the want of a supply which he, a private individual, had at so much hazard sought for their relief, and that when this frontier bulwark was thus destroyed, the fury of the savages would burst like a tempest upon the heads of their own citizens. To these representations, however, the council remained deaf and inexorable; the sympathy for the frontier settlers was deep, but the assistance already offered was a stretch of power, and they could go no farther. The keeper of the public magazine was directed to deliver the powder to Clark; but having long reflected on the situation, prospects and

resources of the new country, his resolution to reject the assistance on the proposed conditions, was made before he left the
council chamber. He determined to repair to Kentucky, and,
as he had at first contemplated, exert the resources of the country for the formation of an *independent state.* He accordingly
returned the order of the council in a letter, setting forth his
reasons for declining to accept their powder on these terms, and
intimating his design of applying for assistance elsewhere, adding,
"*that a country which was not worth defending, was not worth
claiming.*" On the receipt of this letter the council recalled
Clark to their presence, and an order was passed on the 23d of
August, 1776, for the transmission of the gunpowder to Pittsburg, to be there delivered to Clark or his order, for the use of
the people of Kentucky. This was the first act in that long
and affectionate interchange of good offices, which subsisted
between Kentucky and her parent state for so many years; and
obvious as the reflection is, it may not be omitted, that on the
successful termination of this negotiation, hung the connection
between Virginia and the splendid domain she afterward ac-
quired west of the Allegheny mountains.

At the fall session of the legislature of Virginia, Messrs.
Jones and Clark laid the Kentucky memorial before that body.
They were, of course, not admitted to seats, though late in the
session they obtained, in opposition to the exertions of Colonels
Henderson and Campbell, the formation of the territory which
now comprises the present state of that name, into the county
of Kentucky. Our first political organization was thus obtained
through the sagacity, influence and exertions of George Rogers
Clark, who must be ranked as the earliest founder of this commonwealth. This act of the Virginia legislature first gave it
form and a political existence, and entitled it under the constitu-

tion of Virginia to a representation in the assembly, as well as to a judicial and military establishment.

Having obtained these important advantages from their mission, they received the intelligence that the powder was still at Pittsburg, and they determined to take that point in their route home, and bring it with them. The country around Pittsburg swarmed with Indians, evidently hostile to the whites, who would no doubt seek to interrupt their voyage. These circumstances created a necessity for the utmost caution as well as expedition in their movements, and they accordingly hastily embarked on the Ohio with only seven boatmen. They were hotly pursued the whole way by Indians, but succeeded in keeping in advance until they arrived at the mouth of Limestone creek, at the spot where the city of Maysville now stands. They ascended this creek a short distance with their boat, and concealed their cargo at different places in the woods along its banks. They then turned their boat adrift, and directed their course to Harrodstown, intending to return with a sufficient escort to insure the safe transportation of the powder to its destination. This in a short time was successfully effected, and the colonists were thus abundantly supplied with the means of defense against the fierce enemies who beset them on all sides.

The space allotted to this brief sketch, will not admit of a detailed narrative of the adventures of Major Clark after his return to Kentucky. Let it suffice to say, that he was universally looked up to by the settlers as one of the master spirits of the time, and always foremost in the fierce conflicts and desperate deeds of those wild and thrilling days.

Passing over that series of private and solitary adventures in which he embarked after he returned from Virginia, and in which he appears to have taken a peculiar pleasure, but of which no particulars have been preserved, we shall proceed at once to notice his successful expedition against the British posts of Kaskaskia and Vincennes; one of the most important events, if we estimate it by its consequences, immediate and remote, in the early history of the west. It was at the same time marked by incidents of romantic and thrilling interest, and a striking display of the qualities of courage, perseverance, and fortitude, which bring to mind the heroic deeds of antiquity.

The war in Kentucky previous to this time had been a true *border war*, and conducted in the irregular and desultory manner incident to that kind of hostilities. Nearly all the military operations of the period resembled more the predatory exploits of those sturdy cattle-drovers and stark moss-troopers of the Scottish highlands, whose valorous achievements have been immortalized by the graphic pen of the author of Waverly, than the warfare of a civilized people. Every man fought pretty much "*on his own hook*," and waged the war in a fashion to suit himself. He selected his own ground, determined upon the time, place, and manner of attack, and brought the campaign to a close whenever his own inclinations prompted. The war indeed was sustained, and its "sinews supplied," by the adventurous spirit of private individuals. The solitary backwoodsman would sharpen his hunting knife, shoulder his rifle, and provide himself with a small quantity of parched corn as a substitute for bread, and thus equipped for service, start on an expedition into the Indian country, without beat of drum or note of warning. Arrived on hostile soil, he would proceed with the caution of a panther stealing on his prey, until he reached the neighborhood of a village, when, concealing himself in the surrounding thickets, he would lie in wait until an opportunity presented of shooting an Indian and stealing a horse, when he would return to the cultivation of his farm and the ordinary pursuits of his business. Even those more ambitious enterprises which occasionally diversified this personal warfare, were the result rather of the spontaneous combination of private individuals, than of any movement by the state. The perseverance and gallantry of the backwoodsman was left to sustain itself, with little assistance from the power of Virginia, at that time engaged in the tremendous struggle of the war of Independence, which demanded all her energies and taxed all her resources. The state had not disposable means to act on so remote a frontier, nor does she appear to have been distinctly aware of the important diversion of the Indian force, which might be made by supporting the exertions of Kentucky. As little did she perceive the rich temptations offered to her military ambition in the British posts in the west. Yet every Indian engaged on the frontier of Kentucky was a foe taken from the nearer frontier of the parent state. And in those remote and neglected garrisons of Kaskaskia, Vincennes, and Detroit, was to be found the source of those Indian hostilities which staid the advancing tide of emigration, and deluged the whole west in the blood of women and children.

These combined views, however, began to acquire weight with the Virginia statesmen, with the progress of the revolution, and the rapid increase of emigration to Kentucky; and they were particularly aided and enforced by the impressive representations of Major Clark. To his mind they had been long familiar, and his plans were already matured. He was thoroughly acquainted with the condition, relations, and resources of the country, and with that instinctive genius which stamps him as the most consummate of the western commanders, he saw at a glance the policy required to develop the nascent strength and advantages of the infant settlements. At a glance, he discovered what had so long escaped the perspicacity of the Virginia statesmen, that the sources of the Indian devastations were Detroit, Vincennes, and Kaskaskia. It was by the arms and clothing supplied at these military stations that the merciless ferocity of these blood-thirsty warriors was stimulated to the commission of those fearful ravages which "drenched the land to a mire." If they could be taken, a counter influence would be established over the Indians, and the streams of human blood, which deluged the fields of Kentucky, would be dried up.

So strongly had the idea of reducing these posts taken possession of the mind and imagination of Major Clark, that in the summer of 1777 he dispatched two spies to reconnoiter and report their situation. On their return they brought intelligence of great activity on the part of the garrisons, who omitted no opportunity to promote and encourage the Indian depredations on the Kentucky frontier. They reported further, that although the British had essayed every art of misrepresentation to prejudice the French inhabitants against the Virginians and Kentuckians, by representing these frontier people as more shocking barbarians than the savages themselves, still there were to be seen strong traces of affection for the Americans among many of the inhabitants.

In December, 1777, Major Clark submitted to the executive of Virginia a plan for the reduction of these posts. The result was a full approbation of the scheme, and the governor and council entered into the undertaking so warmly that every preliminary arrangement was soon made.

[*We omit here Collins' sketch of the campaign in Illinois, which is more fully recorded in Col. Clark's Letter.*]

Soon after this Louisville was founded, and he made it his headquarters. In 1780 he built Fort Jefferson, on the Mississippi. In the course of this year he led an expedition against the Indians of Ohio, the occasion of which was as follows : On the 1st of June, 1780, the British commander at Detroit assembled six hundred Canadians and Indians, for a secret expedition under Col. Byrd, against the settlements in Kentucky. This force, accompanied by two field pieces, presented itself on the 22d, before Ruddell's station, which was obliged to capitulate. Soon after Martin's station shared the same fate, and the inhabitants, loaded with the spoil of their own dwellings, were hurried off toward Canada.

A prompt retaliation was required, and when Colonel Clark called on the militia of Kentucky for volunteers to accompany his regiment against the Indians, they flocked to his standard without delay. The point of rendezvous was the mouth of Licking river, where the forces assembled. They were supplied with artillery, conveyed up the river from the Falls. When all assembled, the force amounted to nearly a thousand men. The secrecy and dispatch which had ever attended the movements of this efficient commander continued to mark his progress on this occasion. The Indian town was reached before the enemy had received any intimation of their approach. A sharp conflict ensued, in which seventeen of the savages were slain, with an equal loss on the part of the whites. The Indians then fled, the town was reduced to ashes, and the gardens and fields laid waste. Col. Clark returned to the Ohio and discharged the militia, and the Indians, reduced to the necessity of hunting for the support of their families, gave the whites no further trouble that season.

For a long time the ever active mind of Clark had been

revolving a scheme for the reduction of the British post at Detroit, and in December of the year 1780, he repaired to Richmond, to urge the government to furnish him with means to execute this long-cherished design. His views were approved, but before the necessary arrangements could be completed, a British force from New York, under Arnold, carried hostilities into the heart of the State. Clark took a temporary command under Baron Steuben, and participated in the active operations of that officer against the marauding traitor.

After several months had been spent in indefatigable efforts to raise a force of two thousand men, for the enterprise against Detroit, the several corps destined for the service were designated, and ordered to rendezvous on the 15th of March, 1781, at the falls of the Ohio, and Clark was raised to the rank of brigadier general; but unexpected and insuperable difficulties arose, and the ardent genius of the commander was confined to defensive operations. This appears to have been the turning point in the fortunes of the hardy warrior. He had set his heart on destroying the British influence throughout the whole north-western territory. Could he have had the means which he required, his advancement in rank would no doubt have been gratifying; but without a general's command, a general's commission was of no value. Dangers and hardships would have been disregarded; but with his small force to be stationed on the frontier to repel the inroads of a few predatory bands of Indians, when he was eager to carry the war to the lakes, was more than he could bear, and it preyed upon his spirit. From this time forth his influence sensibly decreased, and the innate force and energy of his character languished and degenerated.

He was a lion chained, but he was still a lion, and so the enemy found him in 1782. When the news of the disastrous battle of the Blue Licks reached him, he took immediate measures to rouse the country from that benumbed torpor of anguish and despondency in which this great calamity had plunged it, and to carry the war once more into the enemy's country. In September, a thousand mounted riflemen assembled on the banks of the Ohio, at the mouth of Licking, and moved against the Indian towns on the Miami and Scioto. The Indians fled before them, and not more than twelve were killed or taken. Five of their towns were reduced to ashes, and all of their provisions destroyed. The effect of this expedition was such that no formidable party of Indians ever after invaded Kentucky.

In 1786 a new army was raised to march against the Indians on the Wabash, and Clark, at the head of a thousand men, again entered the Indian territory. This expedition proved unfortunate, and was abandoned.

Several years elapsed before the name of General Clark again appeared in connection with public affairs. When Genet, the French minister, undertook to raise and organize a force in Kentucky for a secret expedition against the Spanish possessions on the Mississippi, George Rogers Clark accepted a commission as major general in the armies of France, to conduct the enterprise. But, before the project was put in execution, a counter revolution occurred in France, Genet was recalled, and Clark's commission annulled. Thus terminated his public career.

General Clark was never married. He was long in infirm health, and severely afflicted with a rheumatic affection, which terminated in paralysis, and deprived him of the use of one limb. After suffering under this disease for several years, it finally caused his death in February, 1818. He died and was buried at Locust Grove, near Louisville.

CLARK'S

Campaign in the Illinois.

Louifville, Falls of Ohio, Novr 19, 1779.

My Dr Sir, continue to favour me with your valuable Leffons; Continue your Reprimands as though I was your fon; when fufpicious, think not that promotion or confer'd Honour will occation any unneceffary pride in me; You have infuf'd too many of your Valuable precepts in me to be guilty of the like, or to fhew any indifference to thofe that ought to be dear to me; it is with pleafure that I obey in tranfmiting to you a fhort fketch of my enterprife and proceeding in the Illinois, as near as I can Recollect, or gather from memorandoms.

After difengaging myfelf from Kentucky, I fet out for Williamfburg in Augt. 1777, in order to fettle my act^s. I had juft Reafons known to few but myfelf that occationed me to refolve not to have any farther Command whatever, without I fhould find a very great call for Troops and my Country

in danger, in fuch cafe I was determined to loofe my
Life rather (*than*) we fhould fubmit. On my arrival at
Town I found to appearance a friend in many gentlemen of note that offered their Intereft to me in
cafe I fhould offer at any Poft. Many was furprif'd
that I would not felicit for fome Birth. I muft
confefs that I think myfelf often to blame for not
makeing ufe of Intereft for my promotion, but to
merit it firft is fuch a fixed principal with me that I
never could, and I hope never fhall afk for a Poft of
Honour, as I think the Publick ought to be the
beft Judge whether a Perfon deferves it or not, if he
did he would certainly be Rewarded according to the
Virtue they had. But finding that we were in (*an*)
alarming fituation, the Indians defperate on one fide,
the Britains on the other, I immediately Refolved to
encourage an Expedition to the Illinois. But to
make it publick was a certain lofs of it. I propof'd
the plan to a few Gentlemen, they communicated it
to the Governour, it was immediately determined on,
to put in Execution as foon as a Bill could be
be paffed to enable the Governour to order it; it
accordingly paff'd, though but a few in the Houfe
knew the real intent of it. After giving the Council
all the intiligence I poffibly could, I refolv'd to pur-
fue my other Plans. But being defired by the Governour to ftay fome time in town, I wated with
impatience, he I fuppofe believeing that I wanted the

Command, and was determined to give it to me; But it was far from my Inclination at that time. I was fummoned to attend the Council-Board, the inftructions and neceffary papers were ready for puting in the name of the Perfon to Command; I believe they expected me to felicit for it, but I refolved not to do fo, for reafons I hinted you before. However, I excepted it after being told the Command of this little Army was defign'd for me. I then got every requeft granted, and (*was*) fully empowered to raife as many Men as I could, not exceeding a certain number,* after being engaged, I was then as Determined to profecute it with Vigour, as I was before indifferent about the Command; I had fince the beginning of the War taken pains to make myfelf acquainted with the true fituation of the Britifh pofts on the Fronteers, and fince find that I was not miftaken in my judgment. I was ordered to Attact the Illinois, in cafe of Succefs to cary my Arms to any quarter I pleafed. I was certain that with five hundred Men I could take the Illinois, and by my treating the Inhabitants as fellow Citizens, and fhew them that I ment to protect rather than treat them as a Conquered People. Engaging the Indians to our Intereft, &c., It might probably have fo great an effect on their Countrymen at Detroyet (they already difliked

---

* For his instructions, public and private, see Appendix.

their Mafter) that it would be an eafy prey for me. I
fhould have mentioned my defign to his Excellency,
but was convinced, or afraid that it might leffen his
efteem for me, as it was a general oppinion that it
would take feveral thoufand to approach that Place.
I was happy with the thoughts of fair profpect of
undeceiveing the Publick refpecting their formidable
Enemies on our Fronteers. I left Williamfburg
January the 18th, made as quick difpatch as poffible
to the fronteers, and by the end of the month had
Recruiting Parties difpofed from Pitfburg to Carolina, had my little Army Recruited in half the time
I expected.

Elivated with the thoughts of the great fervice we
fhould do our Country in fome meafure puting an
end to the Indian War on our fronteers, it may appear
to you to be a mear prefumption in me, but I was
always too jealous of myfelf to be far wrong in plans
that I had fo long ftudied, and fince find that I could
have executed it with the greateft eafe if it had not been
(*the*) following Conduct of many leading Men in the
fronteers, that had like to have put an end to the enterprife, not knowing my Deftination, and through a fpirit
of obftinacy they combined and did every thing that lay
in their power to ftop the Men that had Enlifted, and
fet the whole Fronteers in an uproar, even conde-
fcended to harbour and protect thofe that Deferted; I
found my cafe defperate, the longer I remained the

worfe it was—I plainly faw that my Principal Defign
was baffled — I was refolved to pufh to Kentucky
with what men I could gather in Weft Augufta ; being
Joined by Capt^s Bowman and Helms who had each
raifed a Comp^y for the Expedition, but two thirds
of them was ftopt by the undefign'd Enemies to the
Country that I before mentioned: In the whole I had
about one hundred & fifty Men Collected and fet fail
for the Falls. I had previous to this received Letters
from Capt Smith on Holdfton enforming me that he
intended to meet me at that place with near two hundred Men, which encouraged me much as I was in
hopes of being enabled by that reinforcem^t, at leaft to
attact the Illinois with a probability of Succefs, &c.

I fet out from Redftone the 12th of may leaving
the Country in great confufion, much diftreffed by
the Indians. General Hand, pleafed with my intentions furnifhed me with every neceffary I wanted
and the — of may I arrived at the Canoweay* to the
Joy of the Garriffon as they were very weak, & had
the day before been attacted by a large Body of Indians.

Being Joined by Capt Oharrard's Comp^y on his
way to the Ofark; after fpending a day or two, We
fet out and had a very pleafant Voyage to the falls
of Ohio, having fent Expreffes to the Stations on Ken-

---

* Kanawha River.

tucky from the mouth of the River, for Capt Smith
to join me immediately as I made no doubt but
that he was wateing for me; But you may eafily guefs
at my mortification on being informed that he had not
arrived, that all his Men had been ftopt by the incef-
fant labours of the populace, except part of a Comp^y
that had arrived under the Command of one Captain
Delland, fome on their march being threatened to be
put into Prifon if they did not return; this information made me as Defperate as I was before Determined.

Reflecting on the Information that I had of fome
of my greateft opponents cenfureing the Governour
for his Conduct, as they thought, ordering me for the
protection of Kentucky only; that and fome other
fecret impulfes Occationed me in fpite of all Council
to rifque the Expedition, to convince them of their
error until that moment, fecret to the Principal Officers I had. I was fenfible of the impreffion it
would have on many, to be taken near a thoufand
(*miles*) from the Body of their Country, to attact a
People five times their number, and mercilefs Tribes
of Indians their Allies, and determined Enemies to
us.

I knew that my cafe was defperate, but the more
I reflected on my weaknefs the more I was pleafed
with the Enterprize. Joined by a few Kentuckyans
under Col°. Montgomery to ftop the defertion I knew

would enfue on the Troops knowing their Deftination, I had Encamped on a fmall Ifland in the middle
of the Falls, kept ftrict Guards on the Boats, but
Lieutenant Hutchings, of Dillard's Comp^y, contrived
to make his efcape with his party after being refufed leave to return, luckely a few of his Men was
taken the next day by a party fent after them;
on this Ifland I firft began to difcipline my little
Army knowing that to be the moft effential point
towards fuccefs, moft of them determined to follow me, the reft feeing no probability of making
their efcape I foon got that fubordination as I could
wifh for; about twenty families that had followed
me much againft my Inclination I found now to be
of fervice to me in guarding a Block-houfe that I
had erected on the Ifland to fecure my Provifions.*

---

*There was at this time no settlement at the Falls,
though two thousand acres of the plain on which Louisville
is built, had been patented on 16th of December, 1773, by
John Connelly, a surgeon's mate in the British service. M'-
Murtrie gives the names of five of those who accompanied
Clark and were left on Corn Island, James Patton, Rd. Chen-
owith, John Tuel, Wm. Faith, and J. McManness. After
Clark's departure, they removed to the main land, commenced
clearings, and erected cabins. Other emigrants arrived in the
spring of 1779. The town of Louisville was first laid out
in 1780, by William Pope. *See M'Murtrie's and Casseday's
Histories of Louisville.*

I got every thing in Readinefs on the 26th of June,
fet off from the Falls, double Man'd our Oars
and proceeded day and night until we ran into the
mouth of the Tenefse River the fourth day landed
on an Ifland to prepare ourfelves for a March by
Land; a few hours after we took a Boat of Hunters
but eight days from Kafkafkias; before I would fuffer
them to anfwer any Perfon a queftion, after their
taking the oath of allegiance, I examined them particularly. they were Englifhmen, & appear'd to be
in our Intereft, their intiligence was not favourable, they afked leave to go on the Expedition, I
granted it, and ordered them what to relate particularly, on pain of Suffering, they obferved my in-
ftru6tions which put the whole in the greateft fpirits; Sure by what they heard of fuccefs, in the evening of the fame day I ran my Boats into a fmall
Creek about one mile above the old Fort Miffack;*

---

* The French commander who evacuted Fort Duquesne in
October, 1758, on the approach of General Forbes, descended
the Ohio river and "made a halt about forty miles from the
mouth, and, on a beautiful eminence on the north bank of the
river, commenced a fort, and left a detachment of one hundred
men as a garrison. The post was called 'Fort Massac,' in
honor of the commander, M. Massac, who superintended its
construction. This was the last fort erected by the French on
the Ohio, and it was occupied by a garrison of French troops
until the evacuation of the country under the stipulations of the

Repofed our felves for the night, and in the morning took a Rout to the Northweft, and had a very fatiegueing Journey for about fifty miles, until we came into thofe level Plains that is frequent throughout this extenfive Country. As I knew my Succefs depended on fecrecy, I was much afraid of being difcovered in thefe Meadows as we might be feen in many places for feveral miles; nothing extraordinary happened dureing our Route Excepting my guide* loofeing himfelf and not being able, as we judged by his confufion of giving a Juft account of himfelf; It put the whole Troops in the greateft Confufion. I never in my life felt fuch a flow of Rage to be wandering in a Country where every Nation of Indians could raife three, or four times our Number, and a certain lofs of our enterprife by the Enemie's getting timely notice. I could not bear the thoughts of returning; in fhort every idea of the fort put me in that paffion that I did not mafter for fome time; but in a fhort time after our circumftance had a better appearance, for I was in a moment determined to put the guide to Death if he did not find his way

treaty of Paris. Such was the origin of Fort Massac, divested of the romance which fable has thrown around its name." *Monette's History of the Valley of the Mississippi. Vol.* 1, *p.* 317.

* John Saunders. *Butler's Kentucky, p.* 52.

that Evening; I told him his doom, the poor fellow
fcared almoft out of his wits, begged that I would
ftay a while where I was and fuffer him to go and
make fome difcovery of a Road that could not be far
from us, which I would not fuffer for fear of not
feeing him again, but ordered him to lead on the
party, that his fate depended on his fuccefs; after
fome little paufe he begged that I would not be
hard with him, that he could find the Path that
Evening.   He accordingly took his courfe, and in
two hours got within his knowledge.

On the Evening of the 4th of July, we got within
three miles of the Town Kafkafkias,* having a River
of the fame name to crofs to the Town;   After
making ourfelves ready for anything that might happen, we marched after night to a Farm that was on
the fame fide of the River about a mile above the
Town, took the family Prifoners, & found plenty of
Boats to Crofs in; and in two hours Tranfported
ourfelves to the other fhore with the greateft filence.
I learned that they had fome fufpicean of being attacted and had made fome preparations, keeping out

---

* Kaskaskia, situated on the right bank of the Kaskaskia river,
about seven miles from its junction with the Mississippi, was
settled by the early French explorers a few years after the visit
of La Salle, in 1683, and was the capital of the Illinois country
during its occupancy by the French.

Spies, but they making no difcoveries, had got off
their Guard. ɪ immediately divided my little Army
into two Divifions, ordered one to furround the Town,
with the other I broke into the Fort, fecured the
Governour, Mr. Rochblave in 15 minutes had every
Street fecured, fent Runners through the Town ordering the People on pane of Death to keep clofe to
their Houfes, which they obferv'd, and before daylight
had the whole town difarmed; nothing could excell
the Confufion thefe People feemed to be in, being
taught to expect nothing but Savage treatment from
the Americans. Giving all for loft their Lives were
all they could dare beg for, which they did with the
greateft fervancy, they were willing to be Slaves to
fave their Families. I told them it did not fuit me
to give them an anfwer at that time, they repared to
their houfes, trembling as if they were led to Execution; my principal would not fuffer me to diftrefs
fuch a number of People, except, through policy it
was neceffary; A little reflection convinced me that
it was my Intereft to Attach them to me, according
to my firft Plan; for the Town of Cohos* & St.
Vincents,† and the numerous Tribes of Indians

---

*Cahokia, an old French village, situated in the American
Bottom in St. Clair county, Illinois, a few miles below St.
Louis, and about sixty miles by the river above Kaskaskia.

† Now the town of Vincennes, on the Wabash river, about

attached to the French was yet to enfluence, for I was
too weak to treat them any other way. I fent for all
the Principal Men of the Town who came in as if to
a Tribunal that was to determine their fate forever,
Curfing their fortune that they were not apprifed of us
time enough to have defended themfelves; I told
them that I was forry to find that they had been
taught to harbour fo bafe an oppinion of the Americans and their Caufe: Explain'd the nature of the difpute to them in as clear a light as I was capable of,
it was certain that they were a Conquered People, and
by the fate of War was at my mercy and that our Principal was to make thofe we Reduced free infted of en-
flaving them as they immagined, that if I could have
furety of their Zeal and Attachment to the American
Caufe, they fhould immediately enjoy all the priviledges
of our Government, and their property fecured to
them, that it was only to ftop the farther effufion of
Innocent Blood by the Savages under the influence of

---

one hundred and fifty miles above its mouth. The Indian
village at that point was called Chip-kaw-kay. The French
post was variously designated, by early writers, Post Vincennes,
Post Vincent, St. Vincents, and Au Poste. The fort was
called by the English, Fort Sackville. The name Vincennes
was undoubtedly derived from Francois Morgan de Vinsenne,
who was commandant at the post in 1735.

their Governour, that made them an object of our attention, &c.

No fooner had they heard this than joy fparkled in their Eyes and (*they*) fell into Tranfports of Joy that really furprifed me; as foon as they were a little moderated they told me that they had always been kept in the dark as to the difpute between America & Britain that they had never heard any thing before but what was prejuditial and tended to infence them againft the Americans, that they were now convinced that it was a Caufe that they ought to Efpoufe; that they fhould be happy of an oppertunity to convince me of their Zeal, and think themfelves the happyeft People in the World if they were united with the Americans, and beg'd that I would receive what they faid as their real fentiments : in order to be more certain of their fincerity, I told them that an Oath of fedility was required from the Citizens and to give them time to reflect on it, I fhould not Adminifter it for a few days, in the meantime any of them that chofe, was at liberty to leave the Country with their families, except two or three particular Perfons, that they might repair to their families and conduct themfelves as ufial, without any dread. The Prieft,* that had lately come from

---

* The name of this priest was Pierre Gibault, though Clark, with his characteristic inaccuracy in spelling proper names, calls him *Jeboth*, as will be hereafter seen. Judge Law, in his

Canada had made himſelf a little acquainted with our
diſpute, (Contrary to the principal of his Brother in
Canada) was rather prejudiced in favor of us. He
aſked if I would give him liberty to perform his duty
in his Church I told him that I had nothing to do
with Churches more than to defend them from Inſult.
That by the laws of the State his Religion had as
great Previledges as any other: This ſeem'd to compleat their happineſs.   They returned to their families,
and in a few minutes the ſcean of mourning and diſ-
treſs, was turned to an exceſs of Joy, nothing elſe ſeen
nor heard.   Addorning the ſtreets with flowers & Pa-
vilians of different colours, compleating their happineſs
by ſinging, &c.   In mean time I prepar'd a Detachment on Horſeback, under Capᵗ Bowman, to make a
Deſcent on Cohos, about ſixty miles up the Country; the Inhabitants told me that one of their Towns-
men was enough to put me in poſſeſſion of that place,
by carrying the good news that the People would re-
joice. however I did not altogether chuſe to truſt
them, diſpatched the Captain, Attended by a conſider-
able number of the Inhabittants who got into the

" *Colonial History of Vincennes,*" gives an interesting sketch of
this good man, to whom, he says, " next to Clark and Vigo, the
United States are indebted for the accession of the States com-
prised in what was the original North-Western Territory, than
to any other man."

middle of the Town before they were difcovered; the
French Gentlemen Calling aloud to the People to fubmit to their happier fate, which they did with very
little hefitation: A number of Indians being in Town,
on hearing of the Big Knives, immediately made their
Efcape; In a few days the Inhabittants of the Country took the Oath fubfcribed by law and every Perfon
appeared to be happy; Our friends the Spanyards,
doing every thing in their power to convince me of
their friendfhip, a Correfpondance immediately commenced between the Governour and myfelf. Poft St.
Vincent, a Town about the fize of Williamfburg was the
next Object in my view; as the whole was apprif'd of
me, I was by no means able to march againft it, (their
Governour a few months before going to Detroyet,)
I was refolved if poffible to win their affection which I
thought myfelf in a fair way of doing more fully to
know the fentiments of the Inhabittants about there;
And to execute my Plans I pretended that I was about
to fend an Exprefs to the falls of Ohio for a Body of
Troops to Join me at a certain place, in order to attact
it; it foon had the defired effect. Advocates immediately
appear'd among the people in their behalf. Mr. Jeboth,
the Prieft, to fully convince me of his Attachment
offered to undertake to win that Town for me if I
would permit him and let a few of them go; they
made no doubt of gaining their friends at St. Vincents
to my Intereft; the Prieft told me he would go him-

felf, and gave me to underftand, that although he had
nothing to do with temporal bufinefs, that he would
give them fuch hints in the Spiritual way, that would be
very conducive to the bufinefs.

In a few days the Prieft and Doct^r Lefont, the
Principal, with a few others fet out, and a Proclamation
I fent, for that purpofe, and other inftructions in cafe of
fuccefs. In a few weeks they returned with intiligence
agreable to my wifhes. I now found myfelf in pos-
feffion of the whole, in a Country where I found I
could do more real fervice than I expected, which occationed my fituation to be the more difagreable as I
wanted Men.

The greateft part of my Men was for returning,
as they were no longer Ingaged, furrounded by numerous Nations of Savages, whofe minds had been long
poifoned by the Englifh, It was with difficulty
that I could fupport that Dignity that was neces-
fary to give my orders that force that was neceffary,
but by great preafents and promifes I got about
one hundred of my Detachment Enlifted for eight
months, and to colour my ftaying with fo few Troops,
I made a faint of returning to the Falls, as though
I had fufficient confidence in the People, hoping that
the Inhabitants would remonftrate againft my leaving
them, which they did in the warmeft terms, proving
the neceffity of the Troops at that place, that they
were affraid if I returned the Englifh would again pos-

fefs the Country. Then feemingly by their requeft I agreed to ftay with two Companies of Troops, and that I hardly thought, as they alledg'd that fo many was neceffary; but if more was wanted I could get them at any time from the Falls, where they were made to believe was a Confiderable Garriffon. As foon as poffible I fent off thofe that could not be got to ftay, with Mr. Rochblanch,* and Letters to his Excellency letting him know my fituation and the neceffity of Troops in the Country. Many of the French fond of the fervice, the different Companies foon got Compleat. I ftationed Capt. Bowman at Cohos, Capt. Helms Com^d at St. Vincents Superintendant &c. Domeftick affairs being partly well fettled the Indian Department came next the objeƈt of my attention and of the greateft importance, my fudden appearance in their Country put them under the greateft confternation, they was generally at War

---

*Col. Clark was inclined to treat Mr. Rocheblave, the British commander, leniently, and to restore to him his slaves that had been seized as public plunder. He invited him to dine with himself and officers, with the intention of restoring them; but the violent and insulting language of Mr. Rocheblave on this occasion, entirely frustrated Clark's benevolent designs. The slaves were afterward sold for five hundred pounds which was distributed among the troops for prize money.

In September, 1780, Gov. Jefferson, in a letter to General Washington, mentions a "Lieutenant Governor Rocheblave who has broken his parole and gone to New York." *Jefferson's Works*, vol. 1, p. 258.

againſt us, but the French and Spainyards appearing
ſo fond of us confuſed them, they counciled with the
French Traders, to know what was beſt to be done,
and of courſe was adviſed to come and ſelicit for peace,
and did not doubt but we might be good. Friends; it
may appear otherwiſe to You, but (*I*) always thought we
took the wrong method of treating with Indians, and
ſtrove as ſoon as poſſible to make myſelf acquainted
with the French and Spaniſh mode which muſt be
prefferable to ours, otherwiſe they could not poſſibly
have ſuch great influence among them; when thoroughly
acquainted with it, (*it*) exactly coinſided with my own
idea, and (*I*) reſolved to follow that ſame Rule as
near as Circumſtances would permit, the Kaſkaſkias
Peoreanas & Mechegames immediately treated for
peace; I ſent letters and ſpeaches by Capᵗ. Helms
to the chief of the Kickebues and Peankeſhaws re-
ſiding at Poſt St. Vincents deſireing them to lay down
their Tomahawk, and if they did not chuſe it, to behave like Men and fight for the Engliſh as they had
done, but they would ſee their great father as they
called him given to the Dogs to eat. (gave Harſh
language to ſupply the want of Men; well knowing
that it was a miſtaken notion in many that ſoft
ſpeeches was beſt for Indians) But if they thought of
giving their hands to the Big Knives to give their
Hearts alſo, and that I did not doubt but after being
acquainted, that they would find that the Big Knives

(*were*) of better Principals than what the bad Birds, the
Englifh had taught them to believe. They received the
fpeeches from the Capᵗ, with another of his own, and
after fome Confultation they refolved to take the Big
Knives by the hand and came to a conclufion of
Peace, And faid the Americans muft be Warriers and
no deceivers, or they would never have fpoke as they
did; that they liked fuch People, and that the Englifh
was Liers and they would liften to them no longer;
that by what they had heard the Big Knives, The
Indians had as great a right to fight the Englifh
as they had, that they was convinced that it was the
truth. What they here alluded to was, part of the
fpeech that I had fent to them, explaining to them the
nature of the War in the following manner: That
a great many Years ago, our forefathers lived in
England, but the King opprefed them in fuch a
manner that they were obliged to Crofs the great
Waters to get out of his way. But he not being fatis-
fied to loofe fo many fubjects fent Governours and
Soldiers among them to make them obey his Laws,
but told his Governours to treat them well and to take
but little from them until they grew Populus, that
then they would be able to pay a great deal; By the
good treatment we got, we grew to be a great People and flourifhed faft. The King then wrote to his
Governour & Officers that we had got Rich and numerous enough, that it was time to make us pay tri-

bute, that he did not care how much they took, fo as they left us enough to eat, and that he had fent them a great many Soldiers to make the Americans pay if they refufed, that when they had made the Americans do as they pleafed, they would then make the Indians pay likewife; But for fear the Indians fhould find it out by the Big Knives, that the Englifh intended to make them alfo pay, & fhould get mad with the Englifh for their treatment of their Neighbours the Big Knives, that they, his Governours fhould make us quarrel, &c. We bore their Taxes for many Years, at laft they were fo hard that if we killed a Deer they would take the Skin away and leave us the Meat, and made us buy Blankets with Corn to fead their Soldiers with. By fuch ufage we got Poor and was obliged to go naked; And at laft we complained. The King got mad and made his Soldiers Kill fome of our People and Burn fome of our Villages. The Old Men then held a great Council and made the Tomahawk very fharp and put it into the hand of the Young Men, told them to be ftrong & Strike the Englifh as long as they could find one on this Ifland. They immediately ftruck and Killed a great many of the Englifh. The French King hearing of it fent to the Americans and told them to be ftrong and fight the Englifh like Men, that if they wanted help or Tomahawks he would furnifh them, &c., &c.

This fpeech had a greater effect than I could have immagined, and did more fervice than a Regiment of Men cou'd have done.

It was with aftonifhment that (*we*) viewed the Amazeing number of Savages that foon flocked into the Town of Cohos to treat for peace, and to hear what the Big Knives had to fay, many of them 500 miles diftant, Chipoways, Ottoways, Petawatomies, Miffefogies, Puans, Sacks, Foxes, Sayges, Tauways, Mawmies and a number of other Nations, all living eaft of the Meflicippa, and many of them at War againft us. I muft confefs that I was under fome apprehention among fuch a number of Devils, and it proved to be juft for the fecond or third night, a party of Puans & others endeavoured to force by the Guards into my Lodgings to Bear me off; but was happily Detected and made Prifoners by the elacrity of the Sergent. The Town took the alarm and was immediately under Arms, which convinced the Savages that the French were in our Intereft.

I was determined to follow the Principal that I had fet out upon, let the confequence be what it would. I immediately ordered the Chiefs to be put in Irons by the French Militia. They infifted that it was only to fee whether the French would take part with the Americans or not, that they had no ill Defign; this treatment of fome of the greateft Chiefs among them occationed great confufion among the reft of the Sav-

ages.   The Prifoners, with great fubmiffion, celicited
to fpeak to me, but was refufed.   They then made all
the intereft they poffibly could amongft the other
Indians, (who was much at a lofs what to do as
there was Strong Guards through every quarter of the
Town), to get to fpeak to me; but I told the whole
that I believed they were a fet of Villians, that they
had Joined the Englifh, and they were welcome to continue in the Caufe they had efpoufed, that I was a
Man and a Warrier, that I did not care who was my
Friends or Foes; and had no more to fay to them:
Such conduct Alarmed the whole Town: but I was
fenfible that it would gain us no more Enemies than
we had already, and if they after felicited for terms,
that it would be more fincere, and probably have a
lafting good effect on the Indian Nations; diftruft
was vifible in the Countenance of almoft every Perfon
during the latter part of the day.   To fhew the
Indians that I difregarded them, I remained in my
Lodging in the Town, about one hundred Yards
from the Fort feemingly without a Guard, but I
kept about fifty Men conceiled in a Parlour adjoining, and the Garrifon under Arms; there was great
Counciling among the Savages dureing the Night.
But to make them have the greater idea of my
Indifferency about them, I affembled a Number of
Gentlemen & Ladies, and danced nearly the whole
Night.   In the morning I fummoned the different

Nations to a grand Council, and the Chiefs under guard (*were*) releafed, and invited to Council, that I might fpeak to them in the prefence of the whole. After the common Cerimonies was over, I produced a Bloody Belt of wampom, and fpoke to them in the following manner: I told the Chief that was Guilty, that I was fencible their Nation was engaged in favour of the Englifh, and if they thought it right, I did not. blame them for it, and exhorted them to behave like Men and fupport the Caufe they had undertaken; that I was fenfible that the Englifh was weak and wanted help; that I fcorned to take any advantage of them by Perfuading their friends to defert them; that there was no people but Americans, but would put them to death for their late behaviour; That it convinced me of their being my Enemies. But it was beneath the Character of Americans to take fuch revenge, that they were at their Liberty to do as they pleaf'd, But to behave like Men, and not do any mifchief until three days after they left the town, that I fhould have them efcorted fafe out of the Village, and after that expiration of time, if they did not choofe to return and fight me, they might find Americans enough by going farther. That if they did not want their own Women and Children maffecred, they muft leave off killing ours and only fight Men under Arms, which was commendable; that there was the War Belt, We fhould foon fee which of us would make it the moft

Bloody, &c. Then told them that it was cuftomary
among all Brave Men to treat their Enemies well when
affembled as we were, that. I fhould give them Provifions & Rum while they ftaid, but by their behaviour
I could not conceive that they deferved that appella-
tion, and I did not care how foon they left me after
that day. I obferved that their Countenances and atti-
tude favoured my real defign; the whole looked like
a parcel of Criminals. The other Nations rofe and
made many fubmiffive Speeches excufing themfelves for
their conduct in a very pretty manner, and (*there was*)
fomething noble in their fentiments (their talk I
inclofe), they alledged that they were perfuaded to
War by the Englifh, and made to harbour a wrong
oppinion of the Americans, but they now believed them
to be Men and Warriers, and could wifh to take them
by the hand as Brothers; that they did not fpeak from
their lips only, but that I fhould hereafter find that they
fpoke from their Hearts, and that they hoped I would
pitty their blindnefs and their Women and Children;
and alfo filicited for their Friends that had been Guilty
of the late crime. I told them that I had inftructions
from the Great Man of the Big Knives not to afk
Peace from any People but to offer Peace and War,
and let them take their Choice, except a few of the
worft Nation to whom I was to grant no Peace, for
as the Englifh could fight us no longer he was affraid
our Young Warriers would get rufty without they

could get fomebody to fight, &c. I prefented them
with a Peace & War Belt, and told them to take their
choice excepting thofe who had been Imprifoned. they,
with a great deal of feeming Joy took the Belt of Peace.
I told them I would defer Smokeing the Peace Pipe
until I heard that they had called in all their Warriers,
and then we would conclude the Treaty with all the
Ceremony neceffary for fo important Occafion. they
immediately felicited for fome Perfons to go with them
to be witnefs of their Condu&t, and hoped that I
would favour their Guilty Friends, which I refufed;
and was pleafed to fee them fet trembling as Perfons frightned at the apprehenfion of the worft fate.
Their fpeaker then rofe and made a moft lament-
able fpeach, fuch as I could have wifhed for: Beg-
ing Mercy for their Women and Children: for the
French Gentlemen whom they put the greateft confidence in had given them leffons that favour'd my
Purpofe: I recommended it to them to go to their
father the Englifh, as he had told them that he was
Strong perhaps he might help them as he had promifed;
that they could blame no Perfon but themfelves when
their Nation fhould be given with the Englifh to
the Dogs to eat. When they had tried their Ello-
quence to no purpofe, they pitched on two Young
Men for to be put to death as an attonement for
the reft hoping that would paffify me; It would
have furprifed You to have feen how fubmiffively

thofe two Young Men prefented themfelves for Death,
advancing into the middle of the floor, fetting down
by each other and covering their heads with their
Blankets to receive the Tomahawk (Peace was what I
wanted with them, if I got it on my own terms.) but
this ftroke Prejudiced me in their favour, and for a few
moments (*I*) was fo adjutated that I dont doubt but that
I fhould without reflection (*have*) killed the firft man
that would have offered to have offered to have hurt
them; My wifhes refpecting this Treaty were now
compleat; And I fince find no room to blame myfelf for any omiffion in what followed in the Treaty;
which time has already proved the good effects of it
throughout the Illinois Country.

Our influence now began to fpread among the
Nations even to the Border of the Lakes. I fent
Agents into every Quarter. I continued about five
weeks in the Town of Cohos; in which time I had
fetled a Peace with ten or twelve different Nations.

Being much fatiegued, I returned to Kafkafkias,
leaving Major Bowman to act in which he did himfelf
much Honour. An intamacy had commenced between
Don Leybrau,* Lieut. Governor of Weftern Illinois and
myfelf; he omited nothing in his Power to prove his
Attachment to the Americans with fuch opennefs as left

---

* Don Francisco de Leyba, Spanish Lieutenant Governor
of Upper Louisiana.

no room for a doubt; as I was never before in comp^y
with any Spanifh Gent I was much furprifed in my expectations; for inftead of finding that referve thought
peculiar to that Nation, I here faw not the leaft fymp-
toms of it, freedom almoft to excefs gave the
greateft pleafure; at my return to Kafkafkias I found
everything as well as I could have expected. Having
fo far fixed matters as to have a moment's Leafure,
which was taken up with deeper Reflections than I ever
before was Acquainted with. My fituation and week-
nefs convinced me that more depended on my own
Behaviour and Conduct, than all the Troops that I had
far removed from the Body of my Country: fituated
among French, Spanyards, and Numerous Bands of
Savages on every quarter: Watching my actions, ready
to receive impreffions favourable or not fo of us, which
might be hard to remove, and would perhaps produce
lafting good, or ill effects. It was now that I faw my
work was only begun, maturely examining every circumftance of my paft Actions fixing fuch Refolutions,
that in cafe of misfortune or lofs of Intereft, it fhould
be for want of Judgment only. Strict fubordination
among the Troops was my firft object, and (*I*) foon
effected it. It being a matter of the greateft confequence to Perfons in our fituation. Our Troops being
all Raw and undiffplined You muft (*be*) fenfible of the
pleafure I felt when harangueing them on Perade.
Telling them my Refolutions, and the neceffity of

ftrict duty for our own prefervation, &c. For them to
return me for Anfwer, that it was their Zeal for their
Country that induced them to engage in the Service,
that they were fencible of their fituation and Danger;
that nothing could conduce more to their fafety and
happinefs, than good order, which they would try to
adhere to, and hoped that no favour would be fhewn
thofe that would neglect it. In a fhort time perhaps
no Garriffon could boaft of better order, or a more
Valuable fet of Men. By this time the Englifh party
at Detroit, finding their influence among the Savages
abateing, fent out meffengers through the different
Nations as far as they dare venture. Redoubled their
Prefents and infinuations to little purpofe, as I had a
Number of Perfons well acquainted with the Indians
fpread through the whole that had treated with me, and
Spies continually in and about Detroit for a confiderable time.

One of the Britifh Agents, refiding at Oueaugh,*
about eighty Leagues above St. Vincents hurt our
Growing interefts much, the Indians in that quarter
being inclin'd to defert the Britifh Intereft, but in
fome meafure kept from their good intention by that
Perfon. I refolved if poffible to take him off, and

* Ouatenon, a French settlement on the Wabash, at the
mouth of the Wea (*Oueaugh*): a short distance below where
the town of Lafayette now stands.

fent a Detachment of Men from Kafkafkias under the command of Lieu^t. Bailey, to join Capt. Helms at St. Vincents and if poffible furprife him; the Capt, with about one hundred Men in number, part french Militia and Indians, fet out by water. The Agent hearing of it collected a few Savages from the neighbourhood that he could truft in order to give Battle (the Indians in general Neutrals) but a few days before the Captain's arrival Mr. Celeron thought proper to make his Efcape, leaving his friendly Indians in the Fort, who being Affembled in a Grand Council to determine what was beft to be done, neglecting to fhut the Gate or keep Sentinals (not fuppofing the enemies to be fo near) in the hith of their deliberation Capt. Helms, Bayley, and his fmall Party entered the Fort and ordered them to furrender before they were apprif'd, About forty in number being made Prifoners, the Capt made a valuable Treaty; Gave them their Liberty. this ftroke compleated our Intereft on the Wabache.

St. Vincents being a Poft of great Importance, and not being able to fpare many Men to Garriffon it I took uncommon pains intirely to Attach them to our Intereft as well as the Inhabitants of the Illinois. Knowing no other kind of Government than what might be expected from the luft of Power, Pride and Avarice of the Officers Commanding in that Country, Whofe will was a Law to the whole and certain deftruction to difobey the moft trifleing Command. Nothing could have been more to my Advantage, as I could temper the Government as I pleafed, and every new privilidge appeared to them as frefh Lawrels to the American Caufe.

I by degrees laid afide every unneceffary Reftriction they laboured under. As I was convinced that it was the mercinary views of their former Governours that Eftablifhed them, paying no regard to the happinefs of the People, and thofe Cuftoms Strictly obferved that was moft conducive to good order; I made it a Point to guard the happinifs and Tranquility of the Inhabitants fuppofing that their happy change reaching the ears of their Brothers and Countrymen on the Lakes and about Detroit, would be paving my way to that Place; and (*have*) a good Effect on the Indians. I foon found it had the defired Effect; for the greateft part of the French Gen^t and Traders among the Indians declared for us, many Letters of Congratulation, (*were*) fent from Detroit to the Gen^t of the Illinois, which gave me much Pleafure.

I let flip no oppertunity, in Cultivating our growing Intereft in every Quarter where there was the leaft appearance of a future advantage; and had as great Succefs as I had any right to expect. Great tranquility appeared on every countenance, being apprehenfive that the Britifh Party at Detroit finding it hard to regain their loft Intereft among the Savages would

Probably make a Defcent on the Illinois if they found themfelves Capitulated, for fear of their finding out our Numbers, (parties of Men comeing & going from Kentucky and other places, Recruits, &c.) I fuffered no Parrade except the Guards for a confiderable time, and took every other precaution to keep every Perfon ignorant of our numbers, which was generally thought to be nearly double what we really had. I found that my Ideas, refpecting the movement of the Englifh juft, having certain Accounts by our Spies that Governour Hammilton was on his march from Detroit with a Confiderable Party, taking his Rout up the Meamies river. In a few days receiving certain intiligence that General McIntofh had left Pitfburg for Detroit with a Confiderable Army. Knowing the weaknefs of the Fortifycation of that Poft at that time their numbers, etc., I made no doubt of its being fhortly in our Poffeffion. And that Governour Hambleton, Senfible that there was no Probability of his defending the Fort, had marched with his whole force to encourage the Indians to Harrafs the General on his March; as the only probable Plan to ftop him, little thinking that He had returned, and that Mr. Hambleton had the fame defign on me, that I fuppofed he had at General McIntofch. It being near Chriftmas we feafted ourfelves with the hopes of immediately hearing from Detroit, and began to think that we had been neglected in an exprefs not being fent with the Important news of its being ours.

But a circumftance foon hapned that convinced us that
our hopes was vain.   A young man at the Town of
Cohos holding a Correfpondance and fending Intiligence to Governour Hambleton's Party was Detected
& punifhed accordingly.   By which we Learned the
return of General McIntofch, and Govern' Hambleton's Intentions on the Illinois, But not fo fully
expreffed in the latter as to reduce it to a certainty; but
fuppofing that in cafe of its being true they would make
their firft Defcent on Kafkafkias, It being the ftrongeft
Garriffon and head Quarters.   I kept Spies on all the
Roads to no Purpofe Mr. Hammilton having the
Advantage of Defcending the Oubach and with eight
hundred Men French, Indians and Regulars, took
poffeffion of Poft St. Vincents on the 17th day of
Decem',* he had Parties on the Road that took fome

---

* When Governor Hamilton entered Vincennes, there were
but two Americans there—Capt. Helm, the commandant, and
one Henry.   The latter had a cannon well charged, and placed
in the open fort gate, while Helm stood by it with a lighted
match in his hand.   When Hamilton and his troops got within
good hailing distance, the American officer, in a loud voice, cried
out: "Halt!"   This stopped the movements of Hamilton, who,
in reply, demanded a surrender of the garrison.   Helm ex-
claimed, with an oath: "No man shall enter until I know the
terms."   Hamilton answered: "You shall have the honors of
war;" and then the fort was surrendered, with its garrison of
one officer and one man."—Cutler's History of Kentucky, p. 80.

of our Spies. Hard weather immediately feting in I
was at a lofs to know what to do, many fuppofed that
he had Quit his defign and came no farther than Ome.*
But no Intiligence from St. Vincents, I was ftill under
fome doubt of his being there, except the Com^d had
kept back the Exprefs on account of the High waters.
In this fituation we remain'd for many Days. I
intended to evacuate the Garriffon of Cohos in cafe of a
Siege; But was anctious to have a Conferrence with the
Principal Inhabitants that I knew to be Zealous in our
Intereft, to fix on certain Plans for their Conduct when
in poffeffion of the Englifh, if it fhould be the cafe;
And fet out on the — day of Jan^y, 1779, for that
Town, with an Intention of ftaying but a few days.
Mr. Hammilton in mean time had fent a party of 40
Savages headed by white Men from St. Vincent in
order if poffible to take me Prifoner, and gave fuch
Inftructions for my treatment as did him no difhonour.
This party lay conceal'd keeping a fmall Party near the
Road to fee who Paffed; they lay by a fmall Branch
about three miles from Kafkafkias, there being Snow
on the Ground. I had a Guard of about fix or feven
Men and a few Gentlemen in Chairs, one of them
fwampt within one hundred Yards of the Place where
thefe fellows lay hid, where we had to delay upwards of

---

* Omee, a corruption of *Aux Miamis*, an Indian village at
the confluence of the St. Joseph's and St. Mary's rivers, on the
site of the present city of Fort Wayne, Indiana.

an hour. I believe nothing here faved me, but the
Inftruction they had not Kill me, or the fear of being
overpowered, not having an oppertunity to Alarm the
main Body, (which lay half a mile off,) without being
difcovered themfelves. We arrived fafe at the Town of
Lapraryderush,* about twelve miles above Kafkafkias.
The Gentlemen & Ladies immediately affembled at a Ball
for our Entertainment; we fpent the fore part of the
night very agreably, but about 12 o'clock there was a
very fudden change by an Exprefs Arriving informing us
that Governour Hammilton was within three miles of
Kafkafkias with eight hundred Men, and was determined to attact the Fort that night; which was expected
would be before the Exprefs got to me, for it feems
that thofe fellows were difcovered by a hunter and after
miffing their aim on me, difcovered themfelves to a
Party of Negroes and told them a ftory as fuited
their Purpofe. I never faw greater confufion among a
fmall Affembly than was at that time, every Perfon
having their eyes on me, as if my word was to determine their good or Evil fate. It required but a moment's hefitation in me to form my Refolution, Communicated them to two of my Officers who accompy[d]
me, which they Approved of. I ordered our Horfes
Sadled in order if poffible to get into the Fort before

* La Prairie du Rocher, an old French village, in Randolph
county, on the American Bottom, near the Rocky Bluffs, from
which it derives its name, fourteen miles north-west of Kaskaskia.

the attact could be made. Thofe of the Company that
had recovered their furprife fo far as to enable them to
fpeak, begged of me not to attempt to Return, that
the Town was certainly in poffeffion of the Enemy &
the Fort warmly attacted. Some propofed Conveying
me to the Spanifh Shore, fome one thing and fome
another. I thanked them for the Care they had of
my Perfon, and told them it was the fate of War, that
a good Soldier never ought to be affraid of his Life
where there was a Probability of his doing fervice by
ventureing of it which was my Cafe. That I hoped that
they would not let the news Spoil our Divirfion fooner
than was neceffary, that we would divirt ourfelves until
our horfes was ready, forced them to dance, and endeavoured to appear as unconcerned as if no fuch thing
was in Adjutation. This conduct infpired the Young
Men in fuch a manner that many of them was getting
their Horfes to Share fate with me. But chufing to
loofe no time as foon as I could write a few lines on the
back of my Letter to Captain Bowman at Cohos, I fet
out for Kafkafkias; each Man (*took*) a Blanket, that in
cafe the Fort was attacted, we were to wrap ourfelves in
them fall in with the Enemies fire at the Fort until we
had an oppertunity of getting fo near as to give the
proper fignals, knowing that we would be let in. But
on our Arrival we found everything as calm as we
could expect. The weather being bad, it was then
thought the Attact would not commence until it cleared

up. But no Perfon feem'd to doubt of the Enemies
being at hand, and from many circumftances I could
not but Suppofe it was the cafe, that they defer'd the
Attact for fome time in order to give us time to
Retreat, which I fuppofed they wou'd rather chufe by
their proceedings; But I was determined that they
fhould be difappointed if that was their wifhes. There
was no time loft during the Night, puting every thing
in as good order as Poffible. The Prieft, of all Men
the moft affraid of Mr. Hammilton, he was in the
greateft confternation, determined to Act agreeable to
my Inftruction. I found by his Confternation that
he was fure the Fort would be taken, Except Reinforced by the Garriffon at Cohos which I did not chufe
to let him know would be the cafe although I knew
him to be a Zealous Friend. I pretended that I
wanted him to go to the Spanifh fide with Publick
Papers and Money, the Propofition pleaf'd him well,
he immediately ftarted & getting into an ifland the Ice
paffing fo thick down the Mefficippi, that he was
obliged to Encamp three days in the moft obfcure part
of the ifland with only a Servant to attend him.

I fpent many ferious reflections during the night.
The Inhabitants had always appear'd to be attached to
us but I was convinced that I fhould in the morning
have a Sufficient trial of their fedility (feveral of their
Young Men had turned into the Fort in order to defend
it) but Senfible at the fame time that in cafe they took

Arms to defend the Town that the whole would probably be loft, as I fhould be obliged to give the Enemy
Battle in the Commons. I would have chofe to have
had thofe without families to Reinforce the Garriffon,
and the reft to have lain Neuter.

I refolved to burn part of the Town that was
near the Fort and Guard it, as I knew the greateft fervice we poffibly could do was to Sell the Fort
as Dear as poffible, there being no probability of
efcaping after attact, or expectation of Reinforcements,
as we were too far detached from the Body of our
Country. The only probable chance of fafety was
Capt. Bowman's joining me which I expected the
next evening down the Meflicippi, to defend ourfelves
until Mr. Hamilton's Indians got tired and returned
in four or five Weeks which I expected the greateft
Part would do if they had not that Succefs that they expected. I had no occafion to confult the Garriffon in any
Refolution I fhould fix upon as I knew they was all as
Spirited as I could wifh them to be, and took pains to
make them as defperate as poffible. If You rightly
Confider our Situation & Circumftance You muft conceive it to be defperate; in the morning the firft thing
I did was to affemble all the Inhabitants in order
to know their Refolutions; as they had been the
night Counciling with each other they expected fome
orders Iffued, which I did not chufe to do;
at the Affembly I afked them what they thought of

doing, whether they would endeavour to defend the Town or not; if they did I would Quit the Fort leaving a Small Guard, and head them with the Troops; and if the Enemy lay until the weather Broke, we might probably in the mean time difcover their Camp and get fome advantage of them. They appear'd to be in great confufion, and all my fear was, that they would agree to defend themfelves, and if the Enemy was as numerous as was expected, the whole would be loft. But I need not have been uneafy about that, for they had too maturely ftudied their own Intereft to think of fighting, which they certainly would have done if I had only as many Troops as would have given any Probability of fuckcefs: they difplaid their fituation in fuch a manner as was really moving and with great truth. But denied to Act either on one fide or the other; And begged that I would believe them to be in the American Intereft. But my whole force joined with them would make but a poor figure againft fo confiderable a Party and gave hints that they could wifh us to take Spanifh Protection as they could not conceive we could keep poffeffion a Single day as the Enemy would immediately fet the adjacent Houfes on fire which would fire the Fort (not knowing that I intended to Burn them myfelf as foon as the wind fhifted.) I very feldom found but I could govern my temper at pleafure, But this declaration of theirs and fome other Circumftances put me in a moft violent Rage, and as foon as I could curb my Paffion gave a Lecture fuitable for a fet of Traitors (although I could not conceive the whole of them to be fuch), I ordered them out of the Garriffon, and told them that I no longer thought they deferved favour from me, that I confequently muft conceive them to be my fecret Enemies and fhould treat them as fuch. They endeavoured to footh me into pitty, but to have liftned to them would have deftroyed my intention. I determined to make myfelf appear to them as defperate as Poffible that it might have a Greater effect on the Enemy, (they afked me to iffue an order for all the Provifion in the Town to be brought into the Fort immediately, by which I was convinced that it was their defire that I fhould be able to ftand the Siege as long as Poffible, and only wanted an excufe to the Perfon they expected every moment to be their Mafter, for making the fupplies) I told them that I would have all the Provifions and then Burn the Town to the Enemies hand: that they might fend the Provifions if they chofe it, and fent them out of the Fort: and immediately had fire fet to fome out Houfes. Never was a fet of People in more diftrefs, their Town fet on fire by thofe they wifhed to be in friendfhip with, at the fame time Surrounded by the Savages, as they expected, from whom they had but little elfe but deftruction to expect. The Houfes being covered with Snow, the fire had no effect only on thofe it was fet to, the Inhabitants

looking on without daring to fay a word. I told them
that I intended to fet fire to all thofe that had much
Provifion for fear of the Enemie's getting it. They
were not in fo great a Leathergy, but they took the hint
and before night they brought in fix months Provifions
of all forts; by which they were in hopes to come on
better Terms; but a frefh circumftance Alarmed them.
One of the Inhabitants Riding into the Field, met a
Man that told him he faw a party of the Enemy going
on the Ifland to take the Prieft, he, returning to Town
met the Prieft's Brother in Law and told him what he
had heard, and begged of him not to tell me of it, the
Poor fellow half fcared to death about his Brother,
made all hafte and told me. I took his Evidence, fent
for the Citizen, who could not deny it.

I immediately ordered him hanged. The Town
took the Alarm, hafted about the walls of the Fort, if
poffible to fave their Friend. The Poor fellow given
up to the Soldiers who dragged him to the place of
Execution, each ftriving to be foremoft in the Execution as if they thirfted after Blood; fome was for
Tomahawking him, fome for hanging & others for
Burning: they got to quarreling about it, which at laft
faved his life; the Inhabitants having time to fupplicate
in his favour, but nothing would have faved his life but
the appearance of his Wife and feven fmall Children,
which fight was too moving not to have granted them
the life of their Parent on terms that put it out of his

power to do any damage to me. The weather clearing away Capt. Bowman Arrived the following day with his own and a comp^y of Volunteers from Cohos; we now began to make a tolerable appearance and feemed to defie the Enemy: and fent out Spies on every quarter to make difcovery of them, hoping we might get fome Advantage of them, chufing for many important Reafons to attact them two to one in the field rather than fuffer them to take poffeffion of the Town, which by the form and manner of picquiting, the Yards and Gardens was very Strong. I was convinced that the Inhabitants now wifhed that they had behaved in another manner. I took the advantage of the favourable oppertunity to Attach them intirely in my Intereft, and inftead of Treating them more fevear as they expected on my being Reinforced, I altered my conduct towards them and treated them with the greateft kindnefs, granting them every requeft, my influence among them, in a few hours was greater than ever; they condemning themfelves and thought that I had treated them as they deferved; and I believe, had Mr. Hammilton appear'd we fhould have defeated him with a good deal of eafe not fo numerous but the Men being much better. Our fpies returning, and found the great Army that gave the alarm confifted only of about forty Whites and Indians making their Retreat as faft as poffible to St. Vincents; fent for no other purpofe, as we found after than to take me. We were now fenfible that St.

Vincents was in poffeffion of the Englifh; and confequently we might fhortly expeƈt an Attaƈt though no
danger at prefent, and had fome time to make prepara-
tion for what we were certain of.   I had reafon to
expeƈt a Reinforcement on the prefumption that
Government ordered one on the Receipt of my firft
Letter; ftill encouraged each other and hoped for the
beft: But fuffered more uneafinefs than when I was
certain of an immediate attaƈt, as I had more time to
refleƈt; the Refult of which was that the Illinois in a
few months would be in poffeffion of the Englifh
except the Garrifon which I knew would not be difpofed
to furrender without the greateft diftrefs.   I fent off
Horfemen to St. Vincents to take a Prifoner by which
we might get intiligence, but found it impraƈticable on
account of the high waters; but in the hight of our
anxiety on the evening of the 29th of Jan⁷, 1779
Mr. Vague* a Spanifh merchᵗ, arrived from St. Vin-

---

* Col. Francis Vigo, a Spanish merchant at St. Louis, connected in business with the Governor of Upper Louisiana, as
soon as he heard of Clark's arrival at Kaskaskia, went to him
and tendered him his means and influence, which were joyfully
accepted.   At the suggestion of Col. Clark he started with a
single servant to Vincennes, to learn the actual state of affairs
there.   He was, however, seized at the river Embarrass and
taken before Gov. Hamilton, who released him on parole on
condition that he would report himself daily at the fort.   After
some days, at the earnest solicitation of the inhabitants of the

cents, and was there the time of its being taken, and gave me every intiligence that I could wifh to have Governour Hamilton's Party confifted of about eight hundred when he took poffeffion of that Poft on the 17th day of december paft: finding the Seafon too far fpent for his intention againft Kafkafkias had fent nearly the whole of his Indians out in different Parties to War: But to embody as foon as the weather would Permit and compleat his defign: He had alfo fent meffengers to the fouthern Indians, five hundred of whom he expected to join him only eighty Troops in Garriffon, (our Situation ftill appear'd defperate, it was at this moment I would have bound myfelf feven years a Slave, to have had five hundred Troops) I faw the only

town, by whom Vigo was greatly respected, Gov. Hamilton offered to release him altogether if he would sign an article " not to do any act during the war injurious to the British interests." This he positively refused to do; but he was finally released on agreeing " not to do anything injurious to the British interests *on his way to St. Louis.* He went in a piroque down the Wabash and Ohio and up the Mississippi to St. Louis, thus keeping the *letter* of his bond, but he had no sooner set foot at St. Louis, than he re-embarked and hastened to Kaskaskia, where he arrive'd on the 29th of January, 1799, and furnished Col. Clark with, as he says, "every intelligence I could wish to have." See *Law's Colonial History of Vincennes,* p. 26. Col. Vigo finally settled at Vincennes, where he was still (1834) living at the advanced age of eighty-six, "a venerable and highly-respected citizen." *Butler's History of Kentucky,* p. 80.

probability of our maintaing the Country was to take the advantage of his prefent weaknefs, perhaps we might be fortunate: I confidered the Inclemency of the feafon, the badnefs of the Roads, &c., as an advantage to us, as they would be more off their Guard on all Quarters. I collected the Officers, told them the probability I thought there was of turning the fcale in our favour. I found it the fentiment of every one of them and eager for it. Our Plans immediately concluded on, and fent An Exprefs to Cohos for the Return of Capt. McCarty & his Volunteers, and fet about the neceffary preparations in order to Tranfport my Artillery Stores, &c.

I had a Large Boat prepared and Rigged, mounting two four pounders 4 large fwivels Manned with a fine Comp commanded by Lieut. Rogers. She fet out out in the evening of the 4th of Jan^y (? *Feb^y*) with orders to force her way if poffible within ten Leagues of St. Vincents and lay until further Orders. This Veffel when compleat was much admired by the Inhabitants as no fuch thing had been feen in the Country before. I had great Expectations from her. I conducted myfelf as though I was fure of taking Mr. Hamilton, inftructed my officers to obferve the fame Rule. In a day or two the Country feemed to believe it, many anctious to Retrieve their Characters turned out, the Ladies, began alfo to be fpirited and intereft themfelves in the Expedition, which had great effect on the Young Men.

By the 4th day of Jan^y (? *Feb^y*) I got every thing
Compleat and on the 5th I marched being joined by
two Volunteer comp^ys of the Principal Young Men of
the Illinois Command^d by Capt. McCarty and Fran-
ces Charlaville. Thofe of the troops was Capt^ns Bowman* & William Worthingtons of the light Horfe, we
were Conducted out of the Town by the Inhabitants
and Mr. Jeboth the Prieft, who after a very fuitable
Difcourfe to the purpofe, gave us all Abfolution, And
we fet out on a Forlorn hope indeed; for our whole
Party with the Boats Crew confifted of only a little
upwards of two hundred. I cannot account for it but
I ftill had inward affurance of fuccefs, and never could
when weighing every Circumftance doubt it: But I had
fome fecret check. We had now a Rout before us of
two hundred and forty miles in length, through, I fuppofe one of the moft beautiful Country in the world,
but at this time in many parts flowing with water and
exceading bad marching. my greateft care was to divert
the Men as much as poffible in order to keep up their
fpirits; the firft obftruction of any confequence that
I met with was on the 13th, Arriveing at the two little
Wabachees although three miles afunder they now make
but one, the flowed water between them being at Leaft
three feet deep, and in many places four: Being
near five miles to the oppofite Hills, the fhalloweft

---

* For Captain Bowman's journal of this expedition, see
Appendix.

place, except about one hundred Yards, was three feet. This would have been enough to have ftoped any fet of men that was not in the fame temper that we was.

But in three days we contrived to crofs, by building a large Canoe, ferried acrofs the two Channels, the reft of the way we waded; Building fcaffolds at each to lodge our Baggage on until the Horfes Croffed to take them; it Rained nearly a third of our march, but we never halted for it; In the evening of the 17th we got to the low Lands of the River Umbara,* which we found deep in water, it being nine miles to St. Vincents, which ftood on the Eaft fide of the Wabache and every foot of the way covered with deep water; we Marched down the little River in order to gain the Banks of the main, which we did in about three Leagues, made a fmall Canoe and fent an Exprefs to meet the Boat and hurry it up; from the fpot we now lay on (*it*) was about ten miles to Town, and every foot of the way put together that was not three feet and upwards under water would not have made the length of two miles and half, and not a mouthful of Provifion; to have waited for our Boat, if poffible to avoid it, would have been Impolitic. If I was fenfible that you would let no Perfon fee this relation, I would give You a detail of our fuffering for four days in croffing thofe waters,

---

* The Embarrass river enters the Wabash on the west, a little below Vincennes—course southeast.

and the manner it was done, as I am fure that You wou'd Credit it, but it is too incredible for any Perfon to believe except thofe that are as well acquainted with me as You are, or had experienced fomething fimilar to it. I hope you will excufe me until I have the pleafure of feeing you perfonally. But to our inexpreffible Joy, in the evening of the 23d we got fafe on Terra firma within half a League of the Fort, covered by a fmall Grove of Trees had a full view of the wifhed for fpot (I fhould have croffed at a greater diftance from the Town, but the White River comeing in juft below us we were affraid of getting too near it.) we had Already taken fome Prifoners that was coming from the Town. Laying in this Grove fome time to dry our Clothes by the Sun we took another Prifoner known to be a friend by which we got all the Intiligence we wifhed for: but would not fuffer him to fee our Troops except a few.

A thoufand Ideas flufhed in my Head at this moment. I found that Govr. Hamilton was able to defend himfelf for a confiderable time, but knew that he was not able to turn out of the Fort; that if the Seige Continued long a Superior number might come againft us, as I knew there was a Party of Englifh not far above in the River; that if they found out our Numbers (*they*) might raife the difaffected Savages and harrafs us. I refolved to appear as Daring as poffible, that the Enemy might conceive by our behaviour that

we were very numerous and probably difcourage them.
I immediately wrote to the Inhabitants in general,
Informing them where I was and what I determined to
do defireing the Friends to the States to keep clofe to
their Houfes and thofe in the Britifh Intereft to repair
to the fort and fight for their King; otherways there
fhould be no mercy fhewn them, &c., &c. Sending
the Compliments of feveral Officers that was known to
be Expeted to reinforce me, to feveral Gentlemen of
the Town; I difpatched the Prifoner off with this
letter waiting until near funfet, giving him time to get
near the Town before we marched. As it was an open
Plain from the Wood that covered us; I march'd time
enough to be feen from the Town before dark but
taking advantage of the Land, difpofed the lines in fuch
a manner that nothing but the Pavilions could be feen,
having as many of them as would be fufficient for a
thoufand Men, which was obferved by the Inhabitants
who had Juft Receiv'd my letter, counted the different
Colours and Judged of our number accordingly. But
I was careful to give them no oppertunity of feeing
our Troops before dark, which it would be before
we could Arrive. The Houfes obftructed the Forts
obferving us and were not Allarmed as I expected by
many of the Inhabitants. I detached Lieut. Bayley
and a Party to Attact the Fort at a certain Signal, and
took poffeffion of the ftrongeft Pofts of the Town
with the main Body. The Garriffon had fo little

suspicion of what was to happen that they did not believe the Firing was from an Enemy* until a Man was Wounded through the Ports (which hapned the third or fourth shot) Expecting it to be some drunk^n Indians. The fireing commenced on both sides very warm, a second Division Joined the first. A considerable number of British Indians made their escape out of Town: The Kickepous and Peankeshaws to the amount of about one hundred, that was in Town immediately Armed themselves in our favour and Marched to attact the Fort. I thanked the Chief for his intended service, told him the Ill consequence of our People being mingled in the dark, that they might lay in their quarters until light, he Approved of it and sent off his Troops, appeared to be much elivated himself and staid with me giving all the Information he could.

---

*There is an amusing anecdote connected with the seige, illustrative of the frank and fearless spirit of the times; that while Helm was a prisoner and playing at piquet with Governor Hamilton in the fort, one of Clark's men requested leave of his commander to shoot at Helm's head-quartets, so soon as they were discovered, to knock down the clay or mortar into his apple toddy; which he was sure the Captain, from his well-known fondness for that fine liquor, would have on his hearth. It is farther added, that when the Captain heard the bullets rattling about the chimney, he jumped up and swore it was Clark, and he would make them all prisoners, though the d——d rascals had no business to spoil his toddy." *Butler's History of Kentucky*, p. 80.

(I knew him to be a friend.) The Artillery from the
Fort played brifkly but did no execution. The Garris-
fon was intirely furrounded within eighty and a hundred yards behind Houfes, Palings, and Ditches, &c.,
&c. Never was a heavier fireing kept up on both fides
for eighteen Hours with fo little damage done. In a
few hours I found my Prize fure, Certain of taking
every Man that I could have wifhed for, being the whole
of thofe that incited the Indians to War: all my paft
fufferings vanifhed: never was a Man more happy. It
wanted no encouragement from any Officer to inflame
our Troops with a Martial Spirit. The knowledge of
the Perfon they attacted and the thoughts of their mas-
facred friends was Sufficient. I knew that I could not
afford to loofe Men, and took the greateft care of them
that I poffibly could: at the fame time encouraged them
to be daring, but prudent. every place near the Fort
that could cover them was crouded, and a very heavy
firing during the Night, having flung up a confiderable
intrenchment before the gate where I Intended to plant
my Artillery when Arrived. I had learn that one Ma-
fonville had arived that evening with two prifoners
taken on the Ohio difcovering fome fign of us, fup-
posed (*us*) to be fpies from Kentucky immediately on his
arrival Capt. Lemote (*was*) fent out to intercept them;
being out on our Arival could not gain the Fort; in
attempting feveral of his men was made Prifoners,
himfelf and party hovering round the Town; I was

convinced that they wou'd make off to the Indians at day
brake if they cou'd not join their friends; finding all
endeavours fruitlefs to take him, I withdrew the Troops
a little from the Garriffon in order to give him an oppertunity to get in which he did much to his credit
and my fatisfaction; as I would rather it fhould
Receive that Reinforcement, than they fhould be at
Large among the Savages. The firing again commenced,
A number of the Inhabitants Joined the Troops & Behaved exceeding well in General; knowing of the Prisoners lately taken and by the difcription I had of them
I was fure of their being the Exprefs from Williamfburg
(but was miftaken) to fave the papers and Letters; about
Eight o'clock in the morning I ordered the fireing to
ceafe and fent a flag into the Garriffon with a hand Bill,
Recommended Mr. Hamilton to furrender his Garris-
fon, & fevere threats if he deftroyed any Letters, &c.
He return'd an Anf^w to this purpofe; that the Garriffon
was not difpofed to be awed into any thing unbecomeing
Britifh Soldiers: the Attact was Renewed with greater
Vigour than ever and continued for about two hours. I
was determined to liften to no Terms whatever until I
was in Poffeffion of the Fort, and only ment to keep
them in Action with part of my Troops, while I was
making neceffary preparations with the other (neglected calling on any of the Inhabitants for Affiftants
although they wifhed for it.) A flag appear'd from the
Fort with a Propofition from Mr. Hamilton for three

days Ceffation, A defire of a Conferrence with me
immediately, that if I fhould make any difficulty of
comeing into the Fort, he would meet me at the Gate;
I at firft had no notion of liftning to any thing he had
to fay as I could only confider himfelf & Officers as
Murderers, And intended to treat them as fuch; but,
after fome deliberation I fent Mr. Hamilton my Compliments, and beged leave to inform him that I fhould
agree to no other terms than his furrendering himfelf
and Garriffon Prifoners at difcretion; but if he was de-
firous of a conferrence with me I would meet him at
the Church.   We accordingly met, he Offered to furrender but we could not agree upon terms.   He received fuch treatment on this Conferrence as a Man of
his known Barbarity deferv'd.   I would not come upon
terms with him, and recommend'd to him to defend
himfelf with fpirit and Bravery, that it was the only
thing that would induce me to treat him and his Garris-
fon with Lenity in case I ftormed it which he might ex-
pe&.   He afked me what more I could Require than
the offers he had already made.   I told him (which was
really the truth) that I wanted a fufficient excufe to put
all the Indians & partifans to death, as the greateft
párt of thofe Villains was then with him: all his
propofitions were refuf'd: he afked me if nothing
would do but fighting.   I knew of nothing elfe, he
then begged me to ftay until he fhould return to the
Garriffon and confult his Officers: being indiferent about

him and wanted a few moments for my Troops to re-
fresh themselves, I told him that the firing should not
commence until such an hour, that during that time he
was at Liberty to pass with safety. Some time before a
Party of Warriers sent by Mr. Hamilton against Kentucky, had taken two prisoners, was discovered by
the Kickebues, who gave information of them. A
Party was immediately Detached to meet them which
hapned in the Commons; they conceived our Troops
to be a Party sent by Mr. Hamilton to conduct them
in, an honʳ commonly paid them. I was higly pleased
to see each Party hooping, hollowing and Striking
each other's Breasts as they approached in the open
fields each seemed to try to outdo the other in the
greatest signs of Joy; the Poor Devils never discovered their mistake until it was too late for many of
them to escape: Six of them were made Prisoners, two
of them Scalped and the rest so wounded as we afterwards learnt (*that*) but one Lived. I had now a
fair oppertunity of making an impreffion on the
Indians that I could have wished for; that of convincing
them that Governour Hamilton could not give them that
protection that he had made them to believe he could,
and in some measure to infence the Indians against
him for not Exerting himself to save that Friends: Ordered the Prisoners to be Tomahawked in the face of the
Garriffon. It had the effect that I expected: insted
of making their friends inviterate against us, they up-

braided the Englifh Parties in not trying to fave their
friends and gave them to underftand that they believed
them to be liers and no Warriers. A remarkable Circumftance hapned that I think worthy our notice: An
old French Gent, of the name of St. Croix, Lieut.
of Capt. McGarty's Volunteers from Cohos had but
one Son, who headed thefe Indians and was made Prisoner. The queftion was put whether the White Man
Should be faved. I ordered them to put him to Death,
through Indignation, which did not extend to the Savages. for fear he would make his efcape, his father drew
his Sword and ftood by him in order to Run him through
in cafe he fhould ftir; being painted (*he*) could not know
him. The Wretch on feeing the Executioner's Tomahawk raifed to give the fatal Stroke, raifed his eyes as
if making his laft Addreffes to heaven; Cried, O Save
me. The father knew the Son's voice you may eafily
guefs of the adgetation and behaviour of thefe two
Perfons, coming to the knowledge of each other at fo
critical a moment. I had fo little mercy for fuch Murderers, and fo valuable an oppertunity for an Example,
knowing there would be the greateft felicitations made
to fave him, that I immediately abfconded myfelf: but
by the warmeft felicitations from his father who had
behaved fo exceedingly well in our fervice, and fome of
the Officers, I granted his Life on certain conditions.

Mr. Hamilton and myfelf again met: he pro-
duc'd certain Articles which was refufed, but towards

the clofe of the Evening I fent him the following Articles :

1ft. That Lieut. Governour Hamilton engages to deliver up to Colo. Clark, Fort Sachville as it is at prefent with all the Stores, &c.

2d. The Garriffon are to deliver themfelves up as Prifoners of War and March out with their Arms and Acoutriments, &c., &c.

3rd. The Garrifon to be Delivered up tomorrow, at ten o'clock.

4th. Three days time be allowed the Garrifon to fettle their Accompts with the Traders and Inhabitants of this Place.

5thly. The Officers of the Garriffon to be allowed their neceffary Baggage, &c., &c.

Which was agreed to and fullfilled the next day knowing that Governour Hamilton had fent a Party of Men up the Ouabach to Ome for Stores that he had left there which muft be on their return; I waited about twelve hours for the Arival of the Galley to Intercept them: but fearing their getting Intiligence, difpatched Capt. Helms with a Party in Armed Boats who fuppreffed and made Prifoners of forty, among which was Dejeane, Grand Judge of Detroit, with a large Packet from Detroit; and feven Boats load of Provifions, Indian goods, &c. Never was a Perfon more mortified than I was at this time to fee fo fair an oppertunity to pufh a victory; Detroit loft for want of a few Men;

knowing that they would immediately make greater
Preparations expecting me.   The Galley had taken up
on her paſſage the Expreſs from Williamſburg with
letters from his Excellency.   Having at once all the
intiligence I could wiſh for from both ſides, I was
better able to fix my future Plans of operation againſt
Du Troit.   By his Excellencie's letter I might expect
to have a Compleat Battallion in a few months, the
Militia of the Illinois I knew would turn out, did
did not doubt of getting two or three hundred Men
from Kentucky Conſequently put the matter out oſ
doubt.

I contented myſelf on that Preſumption, having
almoſt as many Priſoners as I had Men.   Seeing the
neceſſity of geting rid of many of the Priſoners, not
being able to guard them; not doubting but my
good treatment to the Volunteers and Inhabitants of
Detroit would Promote my Intereſts there I discharged the greateſt Part of them that had not been
with Indian Parties, on their taking the Oath of Neu-
trility.   They went off huzzaing for the Congreſs and
declared though they could not fight againſt the Americans they would for them, (As I after this had Spies
conſtant to and from Detroit, I learnᵗ they anſwered
every purpoſe that I could have wiſhed for, by preju-
dicing their friends in favour of America.

So certain was the Inhabitants of that Poſt, of
my Marching immediately againſt it, that they made

Provifion for me in defiance of the Garrifon. Many of them has paid dear for it fince.

I difpatched off Capt· Williams and compy with Governour Hamilton,* his Principal Officers and a few

---

* These prisoners were taken to Virginia. " It appeared by papers laid before the Council of State, that Governor Hamilton had issued proclamations and approved of practices, which were marked with cruelty towards the people that fell into his hands, such as inciting the Indians to bring in scalps, putting prisoners in irons, and giving them up to be the victims of savage barbarity. The Council decided that Governor Hamilton was a proper subject for retaliation, and that he should be put in irons and confined in a jail." (*Washington's Writings, vol.* vi, *p.* 317.) The British General Phillips remonstrated against this treatment, as Hamilton had capitulated on honorable terms, Governor Jefferson referred the matter to General Washington, who recommended a mitigation of the punishment. The irons were taken off, but he was still kept in close confinement with the other prisoners. In November, 1799, Mr. Jefferson wrote to General Washington that " Lamothe and Dejean had given their paroles, and are at Hanover Court House. Hamilton, Hay, and four others are still obstinate. They are therefore still in close confinement." (*Ibid, p.* 407.) October 10th, 1780, General Washington wrote : " The State of Virginia, sensible of the dangerous influence which Governor Hamilton holds over the Indians, have absolutely refused to exchange him on any terms, for the present at least." (*Ibid, vol.* vii, *p.* 240.) Governor Hamilton and Major Hayes (*or Hay*) in November, 1780, accepted a parole, and were permitted to go to New York. (*Ibid, p.* 291.) Hamilton was afterwards exchanged,

Soldiers to the Falls of Ohio, to be ſent to Williamsburg, and in a few days ſent my Letters to the Gov-
our[r].

Having matters a little ſetled, the Indian department became the next Objeƈt.   I knew that Mr. Hamilton had endeavoured to make them believe that we
intended at laſt to take all their Lands from them, and
that in caſe of Succeſs we would ſhew no greater Mercy
for thoſe who did not Join him than thoſe that did.   I
indeavoured to make myſelf acquainted (*with*) the Argu-
ments he uſed; And calling together the neighbouring
Nations, Peankeſhaws, Kickepoes, & others that would
not liſten to him Indeavored to undeceive them.   I
made a very long Speach to them in the Indian manner,
Extoll'd them to the Skies for their Manly behaviour
and fedility; told them that we were ſo far from having
any deſign on their Lands, that I looked upon it that
we were then on their Land where the Fort ſtood, that
we claimed no Land in their Country; that the firſt
Man that offered to take their Lands by Violence muſt
ſtrike the tomh[k] in my head; that it was only neces-
ſary that I ſhould be in their Country during the War

and returned to Canada, where, on the recall of Sir Frederick
Haldimand in 1785, he was appointed Lieutenant Governor of
Quebec.   He held this position only one year, when he
returned to England, and was shortly afterwards appointed Gov-
ernor of Dominica.   He died at Antigua in September, 1796.
(*Morgan's Celebrated Canadians, p.* 108.)

and keep a Fort in it to drive off the Englifh, who had a defign againft all People; after that I might go to fome place where I could get Land to fupport Me: The Treaty was concluded to the fatisfaction of both parties: they were much pleafed at what they heard, and begged me to favour them the next day with my Comp^y at a Council of theirs. I accordingly Attended; greateft part of the time fpent in Ceremony, they at laft told me that they had been meditating on what I had faid the day before: that all the Nations would be rejoiced to have me always in their Country as their great Father and Protector: And as I had faid I would claim no Land in their Country, they were determin'd that they would not loofe me on that Account; and Refolved to give me a Piece, but larger than they had given to all the French at that Village, and laying down what they would wifh me to do, &c. I was well pleafed at their offer as I had then an oppertunity to deny the exceptance, & farther convince them that we did not want their Land; they appear'd dejected at my Refufial. I waved the difcourfe upon other Subjects: Recommended a frolick to them that night as the Sky was clearer than ever; gave to them a qun^y of Taffy and Provifions to make merry on and left them. In a few days fome Chipoways and others that had been with Mr. Hamilton, came in and begged me to excufe their blindnefs and take them into favour; after the warmeft Silicitations for Mercy, I told them that the Big Knives

was merciful which Proved them to be warriers; that
I fhould fend Belts and a fpeech to all the Nations; that
they after hearing of it might do as they pleafed but
muft blame themfelves for future misfortunes and dispatched them.   Nothing deftroys Your Intereft among
the Savages fo foon as wavering fentiments or fpeeches
that fhew the leaft fear.   I confequently had obferved
one fteady line of conduct among them: Mr. Hamilton,
who was almoft Deifyed among them being captured
by me, it was a fufficient confirmation to the Indians of
every thing I had formerly faid to them and gave the
greateft weight to the Speeches I intended to fend them;
expecting that I fhould fhortly be able to fulfill my
threats with a Body of Troops fufficient to penetrate
into any part of their Country; and by Reducing
Detroit bring them to my feet.   I fent the following
Speech to the different Tribes near the Lakes that was at
war with us, to-wit:

To the Warriers of the different Nations.

Men and Warriers: it is a long time fince the Big
Knives fent Belts of peace among You Siliciting
of You not to liften to the bad talks and deceit of the
Englifh as it would at fome future day tend to the
Deftruction of Your Nations.   You would not liften,
but Joined the Englifh againft the Big Knives and
fpilt much Blood of Women & Children.   The Big

Knives then refolved to fhew no mercy to any People that hereafter would refufe the Belt of Peace which fhould be offered, at the fame time One of War. You remember laft fummer a great many People took me by the hand, but a few kept back their Hearts. I alfo fent Belts of Peace and War among the nations to take their choice, fome took the Peace Belt, others ftill liftned to their great father (as they call him) at Detroit, and Joined him to come to War againft me. The Big Knives are Warriers and look on the Englifh as old Women and all thofe that Join him and are afhamed when they fight them becaufe they are no Men.

I now fend two Belts to all the Nations, one for Peace and the other for War. The one that is for War has your great Englifh fathers Scalp tied to it, and made red with his Blood; all You that call yourfelves his Children, make your Hatchets fharp & come out and Revenge his Blood on the Big Knives, fight like Men that the Big Knives may not be afhamed when they fight you; that the old Women may not tell us that we only fought Squaws. If any of You is for taking the Belt of Peace, fend the Bloody Belt back to me that I may know who to take by the hand as Brothers, for you may be Affured that no peace for the future will be granted to thofe that do not lay down their Arms immediately. Its as you will I dont care whether You are for Peace or War; as I Glory in War and want

Enemies to fight us, as the Englifh cant fight us any
longer, and are become like Young Children begging
the Big Knives for mercy and a little Bread to eat;
this is the laft Speech you may ever expect from the
Big Knives, the next thing will be the Tomahawk.
And You may expect in four Moons to see Your Women & Children given to the Dogs to eat, while thofe
Nations that have kept their words with me will Flour-
ifh and grow like the Willow Trees on the River
Banks under the care and nourifhment of their father,
the Big Knives.

In a few weeks great Numbers came in to St. Vincents and treated for Peace, being laughed at by thofe
that had ftrictly adheard to their former Treaty with me.
After fixing every Department fo as to promife future
advantage fending Letters to County Lieut. of Kentucky filiciting him to make fome preparatory ftrokes
towards Joining me when called on with all the force
he could Raife, leaving a fufficient Garrifon, on the
20th of march I fet out for Kafkafkias by Water with a
Guard of Eighty men, fpending much time in making
fome obfervation at different Places; confequently arrive
too late to have hindered a War that commenced between
the few Delawares refiding in this part of the World
and the Inhabitants.; a few of them that had joined
the Britifh Party knowing what had hapned went to
Kafkafkias, as was fuppofed to compromife matters;

but getting drunk with fome loofe Young fellows gave fome threats on each fide; one of the Indians fnapping a Gun at a Woman's Breaft, two of them was immediately Killed the reft purfu'd by the Townfmen fome diftance down the River, one Killed and fome others wounded. The War was carried on Pretty equal on both fides for feveral Months: but they at laft thought proper to Silicit a Peace. During my abfence, Capt. Robert George commandˢ the compʸ formerly Capt. Willings, had Arrived from Orleans, taking charge of the Garrifon which was a confiderable Reinforcement to our little Party. Every thing having the Appearance of Tranquility, I refolv'd to fpend a few weeks in Divertions which I had not done fince my Arrival in the Illinois, but found it impoffible when I had any matter of importance in view, the Reduction of Detroit was always uppermoft in my mind, not from a motive of Applaufe; but from the defire I had of Eftablifhing a Profound Peace on our Fronteers; being fo well acquainted with its fituation, Strength, and Influence; that in cafe I was not difappointed in the Number of Troops I expected I even Accounted Detroit my own. Receiving letters from Colᵒ· Bowman at Kentucky informing me that I might expect him to Reinforce me with three hundred Men, when ever I fhould call on him, if it lay in his power, at the fame time receiving Intiligence from Colᵒ· Montgomery, I now thought my Succefs reduced to a certainty, imme-

diately fet about making Provifion for the Expedition
to be ready againft the Arrival of Troops to give the
Enemy as little time as Poffible to compleat the new
fortifications I knew they were then about.

I fent an Exprefs to Col⁰· Bowman, defiring him to
Join me on the 20th of June at St. Vincents with all the
force he Poffibly could raife agreeable to his Letters to
me; fent out Capt·——* among the different nations
of Indians to receive their Congratulations on our late
Succefs receive the fubmiffion of thofe that Refolved
to Defert the Englifh, &c., as well as to get frefh Intiligence from Detroit. The Civil Departmᵗ In the Illinois
had heretofore rob'd me of too much of my time that
ought to be fpent in Military reflection, I was now
likely to be relieved by Col⁰· Jn⁰· Todd† appointed by
Government for that purpofe; I was anctious for
his Arrival & happy in his appointment as the greateft
intimacy and friendfhip fubfifted between us, and on
the — day of may had the Pleafure of feeing him fafely
Landed at Kafkafkias to the Joy of every Perfon.   I

---

*This name is illegible in the manuscript.

† Col. Clark, having desired the Governor of Virginia to
appoint a civil commandant, in October, 1778, an act was passed
establishing the *county of Illinois,* embracing within its boundary
all the chartered limits of Virginia west of the Ohio river. Col.
John Todd, who afterwards lost his life at the battle of Blue
Licks, received the appointment of Civil Commandant and Lieu-
tenant-Colonel of the county.—*Butler's Kentucky,* p. 65.

now faw myfelf happily rid of a Piece of Trouble that I had no delight in. In a few days Col⁰· Montgomery Arrived, to my Mortification, found that he had not half the Men I expected; immediately receiveing a letter from Col⁰· Bowman, with frefh Affurances of a confiderable Reinforcement. The officers in Genˡ· being Anctious for the Expedition, Refolved to Rendevous according to appointment, and if not deceived by the Kentuckyans, I fhould ftill be able to compleat my defign, as I only wanted Men fufficient to make me appear Refpectable in Paffing through the Savages by which means I could on the March Command thofe friendly at my eafe, and defy my Enemies. Three hundred Men being at this time, fufficient to Reduce the Garriffon at Detroit, as the new Works was not compleat, nor could not be accords to the Plan before my Arrival, The Gentlemen of Detroit not being Idle, (having fufficient reafon to be convinced that they were in no danger from the Depᵗ of Pitfburg, always fufpicious of my Attacting them fenfible of my growing Intereft among the favages. In order to give themfelves more time to fortify by making fome divirtion on the Illinois,) engaged a confiderable number of their Savages to make an Attempt on St. Vincents; thofe Indians that had declared for the American Intereft, in order to fhew their Zeal fent word to them that if they had a mind to fight the Boftonians at St. Vincents, they muft firft cut their way through them, as they were Big Knives too. This effectually ftopt their operation; knowing that the Expedition depended intirely on the Kentuckians turning out, I began to be fufpicious of a disappointment on hearing of their Marching againft the Shawnee Towns which proved too true for on my arrival at St. Vincents, the firft of July, inftead of two or three hundred men that I was promifed, I found only about thirty Volunteers, meeting with a Repulfe from the Shawnees* got difcouraged Confequently not in the power of the Com^d to March them as Militia, being for fome time (as I hinted before) fufpitious of a difappointment, I had conducted matters fo as to make no Ill impreffion on the minds of the Savages in cafe I fhould not proceed, as the whole had fufpected that my defign was againft Detroit; Several Nations filicited me to go and fuffer them to Join me. Various was the conjectures refpecting to the Propriety of the Attempt with the Troops we had (about three hund^d & fifty), at a Council of War held for the purpofe there was only

---

*"Col. Bowman carried on an expedition against the Shawnese at old Chillicothe, with one hundred and sixty men, in July, 1779. Here they arrived undiscovered, and a battle ensued, which lasted until ten o'clock A. M., when Col. Bowman, finding he could not succeed at this time, retreated about thirty miles. The Indians, in the meantime, collecting all their forces, pursued and overtook him, when a smart fight continued near two hours, not to the advantage of Col. Bowman's party." *Boone's Narrative*, in *Imlay's Western Territory*, London, 1797, p. 35^2.

two cafting voices againft it, and I pretend it was on account of Gen¹ Sullivant's Marching on Niagary, which we Juft heard that ftopt us, that there was no doubt of his fuccefs. Detroit would fall of courfe; and confequently was not worth our while Marching againft it: although I knew at the fame time Detroit would not fall with Niagary, as they had an eafy communication with Montreal through another Channel, by way of the Grand River. A number of Indians vifited me at this time renewing the Chain of friendfhip &c.; To all of whom I gave Gen¹ fatisfaction, except that of my refutial of a Tract of Land that their Chief had formerly offered me. I inquired of feveral Gentlemen acquainted with them, why they were Silicitus about it; their oppinions was that the Indians being exceedingly Jealous of their Lands being taken without their Confent, being told by the Englifh that I had a defign on their Country, by my exceping a Tract from them as a preasent, would prove fufficiently to them that what they had been told was falfe, being fatisfyed in this they alfo had a defire of my Remaining in their Country as their Chief and Guardian and that my refufial had given them fufpicion; in order to Remove it I made a fuitable Speech to them which gave Gen¹ fatisfaction and in a few days they with a great deal of Ceremony prefented me the following Deed of gift:

By the TOBACOES SON, *Grand Chief of all the Peankeſhaws Nations and of all the Tribes, Grand Dore to the Ouabache as ordered by the Maſter of Life, holding the Tomahawk in one hand and Peace in the other: Judging the Nations, giving entrance for thoſe that are for Peace, and making them a clear road, &c.*

DECLARATION.

WHEREAS for many Years paſt, this once Peaceable Land hath been put in confuſion by the Engliſh encouraging all People to Raiſe the Tommahawk Againſt the Big Knives, ſaying that they were a bad People, Rebellious, and ought to be put from under the Sun, and their names to be no more.

But as the Sky of our Councils was always Miſty, and never Clear we ſtill was at a loſs to know what to do, hoping that the Maſter of Life would one Day or other make the Sky Clear and put us in the right Road. He taking Pitty on us ſent a father among us (Colº. George Rogers Clark) that has cleared our eyes And made our Paths ſtraight defending our Lands, &c., So that we now enjoy Peace from the Riſing to the Setting of Sun; and the Nations even to the heads of the great River (meaning the Meſſicippi) are happy and will no more liſten to Bad Birds; but abide by the Councils of their great father, A Chief of the Big Knives that is now among us.

AND whereas it is our defire that he fhould long remain among us, that we may take his Council and be happy, it alfo being our defire to give him Lands to refide on in our Country that we may at all times fpeak to him. After many Silicitations to him to make choice of a Tract, he chufing the Lands adjoining the falls of Ohio on the weft fide of faid River.

I do hereby in the names of all the Great Chiefs and Warriers of the Ouabafh and their Allies, Declare that fo much Lands at the falls of Ohio contained in the following bounds, to-wit, Begining oppofite the middle of the firft Ifland below the falls, Bounded upwards by the weft Bank of the River fo far as to include two Leagues and half on a ftraight line from the begining, thence at right angles with faid line two Leagues & half in Breadth, in all its Parts fhall hereafter and ever be the fole property of our great father (Colo. Clark) with all things thereto belonging, either above or below the Earth fhall be and is his ; except a Road through faid Land to his Door, which fhall remain ours, and for us to walk on to fpeak to our father. All Nations from the Rifing to the feting of the Sun, that are not in alliance with us are hereby warned to efteem the faid gift as facred and not to make that Land tafte of Blood ; that all People either at peace or War may repair in fafety to get Council of our father. Whoever firft darkens that Land fhall no longer have a Name. This declaration fhall forever be a Witnefs between all

Nations and our Prefent G^t father; that the faid Lands
are forever hereafter his Property.   In witnefs whereof
I do in the name of all the Great Chiefs and Warriers of the Ouabafh in open Council affix my mark
and Seal done at St. Vincents this 16th day of June
1779.

(Signed) FRANCIS SON OF TOBACCO.

Which Deed, I excepted, and Indeavoured to convince
them how much I Prifed fo liberal a gift &c as I had
no Idea of haveing Property in the Lands myfelf,
knowing the Laws of my Country Juftly againft it; I
chofe it at the falls of Ohio fufpecting that I might
hereafter find it neceffary to fortify that Place for the
conveniency of free Intercourfe.   Having a Number of
fupernumery Officers I fent them Into the Settlement
Recruiting, finding the Intereft of the Department required me to fpend a few months at the Falls of Ohio
being alfo Induced with the hopes of giving the Shaw-
neefs a Drubing in cafe a fufficient force Could be
again raifed at Kentucky; After giving proper Inftruction for the direction of the Com^ds of the different
Pofts I fet out for the falls where I Arrived fafe on the
20th day of Auguft.   I received an Exprefs from his
Excellency much to my Satisfaction having frefh
Affurance of a fufficient Reinforcement and his Intention of Errecting a Fortification at or near the mouth

of Ohio,* fo much the defire of every Perfon it being a Place of great Importance, and by having a Strong fortification &c it would immediately be the Mart and Key of the Weftern Country; all my Expectations in my being here has been difappointed (except laying up a confiderable quantity of Beef) by lownefs of the Ohio which (*is*) fo remarkable that it would be worth Recording, few being able to navagate it with the fmalleft Canoes for feveral months Paft.

I fhall not for the future leave it in Your Power to accufe me for a Neglect of friendfhip, but fhall continue to tranfmit to You whatever I think worth Your notice.

I am Sir with Efteem Yours.

N. B. As for the defcription of the Illinois Country which you feem fo anctious for you may expect to have by the enfuing fall as I expect by that

---

* "In 1780, Col. Clark descended the Ohio from the Rapids with his Virginia regiment, and established Fort Jefferson at the point where the line of latitude of thirty-six degrees thirty minutes strikes the left bank of the Mississippi. The Chickasaw Indians then had title to the country west of the Tennessee and were exasperated by such a movement of apparent hostility. Between that tribe and the colonies an unbroken friendship had existed during the war of the Revolution, which it was exceedingly important to preserve. The fort was abandoned therefore, as soon as their dissatisfaction was known, and the immediate consequence was, the restoration of their attachment and confidence." *Morehead's Address, p.* 84.

Period to be able to give you a more Gen¹ Idea of it.
this You may take for granted that its more Beautiful
than any Idea I could have formed of a Country almoſt
in a ſtate of Nature, every thing you behold is an Additional Beauty; On the River You'll find the fineſt
Lands the Sun ever ſhone on; In the high Country
You will find a Variety of Poor & Rich Lands with
large Meadows extending beyond the reach of Your
Eyes Varigated with groves of Trees appearing like
Iſlands in the Seas, covered with Buffloes and other
Game; in many Places with a good Glaſs You may ſee
all thoſe that is on their feet in half a Million of Acres;
ſo level is the Country, which ſome future day will
excell in Cattle.   The Settlements of the Illinois commenced about one hundred Years ago by a few Traders
from Canada.   my Reflections on that head its citu-
ation the probability of a flouriſhing Trade the ſtate
of the Country at Preſent what its capable of Produc-
ing, My oppinion Reſpecting the cauſe of thoſe extenfive Plains &c, the Advantages ariſing by ſtrong fortifications and Settlements at the mouth of Ohio.   The
different Nations of Indians, their Traditions, Numbers,
&c., you may expect in my next.

G. R. CLARK.

APPENDIX.

A.

Instructions to Colonel Clark.

(PUBLIC.)

LIEUT. COLONEL GEORGE ROGERS CLARK:

You are to proceed, without loss of time, to enlist seven companies of men, officered in the usual manner, to act as militia under your own orders. They are to proceed to Kentucky, and there to obey such orders and directions as you shall give them, for three months after their arrival at that place ; but to receive pay, etc., in case they remain on duty a longer time.

You are empowered to raise these men in any county in the Commonwealth ; and the county lieutenants, respectively, are requested to give all possible assistance in that business.

Given under my hand at Williamsburgh, January 2, 1778.

P. HENRY.

(PRIVATE.*)

VIRGINIA SCt.

In Council, Wmsbug, Jan. 2, 1778.

LIEUT. COLONEL GEORGE ROGERS CLARK:

You are to proceed with all convenient Speed to raise Seven Companies of Soldiers to consist of fifty men each officered in the usual manner & armed most properly for the Enterprise, & with this Force attack the British post at Kaskasky.

It is conjectured that there are many pieces of Cannon & military Stores to considerable amount at that place, the taking & preservation of which would be a valuable acquisition to the State. If you are so fortunate therefore as to succeed in your Expectation, you will take every possible Measure to secure the artillery & stores & whatever may advantage the State.

For the Transportation of the Troops, provisions, &c., down the Ohio, you are to apply to the Commanding Officer at Fort Pitt for Boats, &c. during the whole Transaction you are to take especial Care to keep the true Destination of your Force secret. Its success depends upon this. Orders are therefore given to Captn Smith to secure the two men from Kaskasky. Similar conduct will be proper in similar cases.

It is earnestly desired that you show Humanity to such British Subjects and other persons as fall in your hands. If the white Inhabitants at the post & the neighbourhood will give undoubted Evidence of their attachment to this State (for it is certain they live within its Limits) by taking the Test prescribed by Law and

---

* From a *fac-simile* copy of the original.

by every other way & means in their power, Let them be treated as fellow Citizens & their persons & property duly secured. Assistance & protection against all Enemies whatever shall be afforded them, & the commonwealth of Virginia is pledged to accomplish it. But if these people will not accede to these reasonable Demands, they must feel the Miseries of War, under the direction of that Humanity that has hitherto distinguished Americans, & which it is expected you will ever consider as the Rule of your Conduct, & from which you are in no Instance to depart.

The Corps you are to command are to receive the pay & allowance of Militia & to act under the Laws & Regulations of this State now in Force as Militia. The Inhabitants at this Post will be informed by you that in Case they accede to the offers of becoming Citizens of this Commonwealth a proper Garrison will be maintained among them & every Attention bestowed to render their Commerce beneficial, the fairest prospects being opened to the Dominions of both France & Spain.

It is in Contemplation to establish a post near the Mouth of Ohio. Cannon will be wanted to fortify it. Part of those at Kaskasky will be easily brought thither or otherwise secured as circumstances will make necessary.

You are to apply to General Hand for powder & Lead necessary for this Expedition. If he can't supply it the person who has that which Capt Lynn bro^t from Orleans can. Lead was sent to Hampshire by my orders & that may be delivered you. Wishing you success, I am

Sir,

Your h'ble Serv.,

P. Henry.

B.

Major Bowman's Journal.

From Louisville Literary News-Letter, Nov. 21, 1840.

"We publish below a journal of the expedition of General Clark against the British post at Vincennes in 1779, commencing with his march from Kaskaskia. It was kept by Joseph Bowman, one of the Captains in the expedition, and is referred to by Mr. Butler in his "History of Kentucky" as "*Major Bowman's Journal,*" the writer having subsequently held the rank of Major. At the time where this journal commences, Clark was in possession of Kaskaskia and Cahokia. Vincennes had once been gained over to him through the influence of a French priest, M. Gibault; but as Clark had not soldiers to spare sufficient to maintain a garrison there, it had been retaken by Gov. Hamilton. The journal will explain the sequel.

The orignal manuscript of this journal—much effaced, and in some places illegible—is in possession of the Kentucky Historical Society. The Vincennes Historical and Antiquarian Society have a copy, which we transcribed for them and for the use of our friend Judge Law of that place."

JOURNAL OF THE PROCEEDINGS OF COL. GEO. R. CLARK, FROM 27TH JANUARY, 1779, TO MARCH 20TH INST.

M. Vigo, a Spanish subject, who has been at Post St. Vincents on his lawful business, arrived and gave us intelligence that Gov. Hamilton, with thirty regulars and fifty volunteers and about 400 Indians, had arrived in November and taken that Post with Capt. Helm and such other Americans who were there with arms, * * (*two or three words illegible*) * * and disarmed the settlers and inhabitants. On which Col. Clark called a council of his officers, and it was concluded to go and attack Gov. Hamilton at St. Vincents; for fear, if it was let alone till Spring, that he, with all the force that he could bring, would cut us off * * (*a part of a leaf is here torn off from the* MS.)

Jan. 31*st.* Sent an express to Cahokia for volunteers and other extraordinary things.

Feb. 1. Orders given for a large batteau to be repaired and provisions got ready for the expedition concluded on.

2*d.* A pack-horse master appointed and ordered to prepare pack-saddles, &c., &c.

3*d.* The galley or batteau finished—called her the *Willing.* Put her loading on board, together with two four-pounders and four swivels, ammunition, &c., &c.

4*th.* About 10 o'clock Capt. McCarty arrived with a company of volunteers from Cahokia; and about two o'clock in the (*after*) noon, the batteau set off under the command of Lieut. Rogers, with forty-six men, with orders to proceed to a certain station near St. Vincents, till farther orders.

5*th.* Raised another company of volunteers, under the

command of Capt. Francis Charleville, which, added to our force, increased our number to 170 men * * (*torn off*) * * artillery, pack-horses, men, &c.; about 3 o'clock we crossed the Kaskaskia with our baggage and marched about a league from town. Fair and drizzly weather. Began our march early. Made a good march for about nine hours, the road very bad, with mud and water. Pitched our camp in a square, baggage in the middle; every company to guard their own squares.

8th. Marched early through the waters, which we now began to meet in those large and level plains, where, from the flatness of the country, (*the water*) rests a considerable time before it drains off. Notwithstanding which our men were in great spirits, though much fatigued.

9th. Made another day's march. Fair the part of the day.

10th. Crossed the river of the Petit Fork upon trees that were fell for that purpose. The water being so high there was no fording it,—still raining and no tents—encamped near the river. Stormy weather.

11th. Crossed the Saline river. Nothing extraordinary this day.

12th. Marched across Cot plains; saw and killed numbers of buffaloes. The road very bad from the immense quantity of rain that had fallen. The men much fatigued. Encamped on the edge of the woods. This plain or meadow being fifteen or more miles across, it was late in the night before the baggage and troops got together. Now twenty-one miles from St. Vincents.

13th. Arrived early at the two Wabashes. Although a

league asunder they now made but one. We set to making a canoe.

14*th*. Finished the canoe and put her into the river about 4 o'clock in the afternoon.

15*th*. Ferried across the two Wabashes, it being then five miles in water to the opposite hills, where we encamped. Still raining. Orders not to fire any guns for the future but in case of necessity.

16*th*. Marched all day through rain and water, crossed Fox river. Our provisions began to be short.

17*th*. Marched early—crossed several runs, very deep. Sent Mr. Kennedy, our commissary, with three men, to cross the river Embarras, if possible, and proceed to a plantation opposite Port St. Vincents, in order to steal boats or canoes to ferry us across the Wabash. About an hour by sun we got near the river Embarras. Found the country all overflown with water. We strove to find the Wabash. Traveled till 8 o'clock in mud and water, but could find no place to encamp on. Still kept marching on. But after some time Mr. Kennedy and his party returned. Found it impossible to cross Embarras river. We found the water falling from a small spot of ground ; staid there the remainder of the night. Drizzly and dark weather.

18*th*. At break of day heard Gov. Hamilton's morning gun. Set off and marched down the river. Saw some fine land. About two o'clock came to the bank of the Wabash ; made rafts for four men to cross and go up to town and steal boats. But they spent day and night in the water to no purpose, for there was not one foot of dry land to be found.

19*th*. Capt. McCarty's company set to making a canoe ; and at 3 o'clock the four men returned after spending the night on some old logs in the water. The canoe finished, Capt. McCarty with three of his men embarked in the canoe and made the third attempt to steal boats. But he soon returned, having discovered four large fires about a league distant from our camp, which seemed to him to be fires of whites and Indians. Immediately Col. Clark sent two men in the canoe, down to meet the batteau, with orders to come on day and night; that being our last hope, and (we) starving. Many of the men much cast down, particularly the volunteers. No provisions of any sort, now two days. Hard fortune!

20th. Camp very quiet but hungry; some almost in despair; many of the Creole volunteers talking of returning. Fell to making more canoes, when, about 12 o'clock, our centry on the river brought to a boat with five Frenchmen from the Post, who told us we were not as yet discovered, that the inhabitants were well disposed towards us, &c. Capt. Willing's brother, who was taken in the fort, had made his escape to us. And that one Masonville, with a party of Indians, were then seven days in pursuit of him, with much news,—more news to our favor, such as repairs done the fort, the strength, &c., &c. They informed us of two canoes they had adrift some distance above us. Ordered that Capt. Worthington, with a party, go in search of them. Returned late with one only. One of our men killed a deer, which was brought into the camp. Very acceptable.

21st. At break of day began to ferry our men over in our two canoes to a small hill called the Momib or Bubbriss. Capt. Williams, with two men, went to look for a passage and were discovered by two men in a canoe, but could not fetch them to. The whole army being over, he thought to get to town that night, so plunged into the water sometimes to the neck, for more than one league, when we stopped on the next hill of the same name, there being no dry land on any side for many leagues. Our pilots say we cannot get along, that it is impossible. The whole army being over we encamped. Rain all this day—no provisions.

22*d.* Col. Clark encourages his men, which gave them great spirits. Marched on in the waters. Those that were weak and famished from so much fatigue, went in the canoes. We came one league farther to some sugar camps, where we stayed all night. Heard the evening and morning guns from the fort. No provisions yet. Lord help us !

23*d.* Set off to cross the plain called Horse-shoe Plain, about four miles long, all covered with water breast high. Here we expected some of our brave men must certainly perish, having froze in the night, and so long fasting. Having no other resource but wading this plain, or rather lake, of waters, we plunged into it with courage, Col. Clark, being first,* taking care to have the

---

*Without food, benumbed with cold, up to their waists in water covered with broken ice, the men composing Clark's troops and at one time mutinied, refused to march. All the persuasions of Clark had no effect on the half-starved and half-frozen soldiers. In one of the companies was a small boy who acted as drummer. In the same company was a sergeant, standing six feet two inches in his stockings, stout, athletic, and devoted to Clark. Finding that his eloquence had no effect upon the men, in persuading them to continue their line of march, Clark mounted the little drummer on the shoulders of the stalwart sergeant, and gave orders to him to plunge into the half-frozen water. He did so, the little drummer beating the *charge* from his lofty perch, while Clark, with sword in hand, followed them giving the command as he threw aside the floating ice—" FORWARD !" Elated and amused with the scene, the men promptly obeyed, holding their rifles above their heads, and in spite of all obstacles, reached the high land beyond them safely. *Law's Vincennes, p.* 32.

boats try to take those that were weak and numbed with the cold into them. Never were men so animated with the thought of avenging the wrongs done to their back settlements, as this small army was.

About one o'clock we came in sight of the town. We halted on a small hill of dry land called Warren's Island, where we took a prisoner hunting ducks, who informed us that no person suspected our coming at that season of the year. Col. Clark wrote a letter by him to the inhabitants, in the following manner:

To the Inhabitants of Post St. Vincents:

GENTLEMEN:—Being now within two miles of your village with my army, determined to take your Fort this night, and not being willing to surprise you, I take this method to request such of you as are true citizens, and willing to enjoy the liberty I bring you, to remain still in your houses. And those, if any there be, that are friends to the King, will instantly repair to the fort and join the *Hair-buyer General,** and fight like men. And if any such, as do not go to the Fort shall be discovered afterwards, they may depend on severe punishment. On the contrary, those that are true friends to liberty, may depend on being well treated. And I once more request them to keep out of the streets; for every one I find in arms on my arrival, I shall treat as an enemy.

(Signed,)   G. R. CLARK.

In order to give time to publish this letter, we lay still till

---

* Alluding to the fact that Gov. Hamilton had offered rewards for the scalps of Americans.

about sundown, when we began our march all in order, with colours flying and drums braced. After wading to the edge of the water breast high, we mounted the rising ground the town is built on about 8 o'clock. Lieut. Bayley, with fourteen regulars, was detached to fire on the Fort, while we took possession of the town, and ordered to stay till he was relieved by another party, which was soon done. Reconnoitered about to find a place to throw up an entrenchment. Found one, and set Capt. Bowman's company to work. Soon crossed the main street, about one hundred and twenty yards from the first gate. We were informed that Capt. Lamath, with a party of twenty-five men, were out on a scout, who heard our firing and came back. We sent a party to intercept them, but missed them. However, we took one of their men, and one Capt. Maison Ville, a principal man; the rest making their escape under the cover of the night into the fort. The cannon played smartly. Not one of our men wounded. Men in the Fort badly wounded. Fine sport for the sons of Liberty.

24th. As soon as daylight, the Fort began to play her small arms very briskly. One of our men got slightly wounded. About 9 o'clock the Colonel sent a flag with a letter to Governor Hamilton. The firing then ceased, during which time our men were provided with a breakfast, it being the only meal of victuals since the 18th inst.

Col. Clark's Letter as follows:

" *Sir :* —In order to save yourself from the impending storm that now threatens you, I order you immediately to surrender yourself, with all your garrison, stores, &c., &c., &c. For if I am obliged to storm, you may depend on such treatment is as justly due to a murderer. Beware of destroying stores of any

kind, or any papers, or letters, that are in your possession ; for, by Heavens, if you do, there shall be no mercy shown you.
      (Signed)   G. R. CLARK."

Answer from Gov. Hamilton.
    " GOVERNOR HAMILTON begs leave to acquaint Col. Clark, that he and his garrison are not disposed to be awed into an action unworthy of British subjects."

    The firing then began very hot on both sides. None of our men wounded; several of the men in the Fort wounded through the port holes, which caused Governor Hamilton to send out a flag with the following letter :

    ".GOVERNOR HAMILTON proposes to Col. Clark a truce for three days; during which time he proposes there shall be no defensive work carried on in the garrison, on condition that Col. Clark shall observe, on his part, a like cessation of any offensive work. That is, he wishes to confer with Col. Clark as soon as can be ; and promises, that whatever may pass between them two and another person mutually agreed upon to be present, shall remain secret till matters be finished, as he wishes that whatever the result of their conference, it may be to the honour and credit of each party. If Col. Clark makes a difficulty of coming into the fort, Lieut. Gov. Hamilton will speak to him by the gate.
      (Signed)   HENRY HAMILTON.
    24th Feb., '79."

Col. Clark's Answer.

" COL. CLARK's compliments to Gov. Hamilton, and begs to inform him that he will not agree to any other terms than that of Mr. Hamilton's surrendering himself and garrison prisoners at discretion. If Mr. Hamilton is desirous of a conference with Col. Clark, he will meet him at the church with Capt. Helm.

G. R. C.

Feb. 24, '79."

The messenger returned with the above answer, during which time came a party of Indians down the hill behind the town, who had been sent by Gov. Hamilton to get some scalps and prisoners from the falls of the Ohio. Our men having got news of it, pursued them, killed two on the spot, wounded three, took six prisoners; brought them into town. Two of them proving to be white men, that they took prisoners, we released them, and brought the Indians to the main street before the Fort gate, there tomahawked them, and threw them into the river; during which time Col. Clark and Governor Hamilton met at the church. Governor Hamilton produced certain articles of capitulation, with his name signed to them, which were refused. The Colonel told him he would consult with his officers and let him know the terms he would capitulate on. Terms as follows:

1. That Lieut. Col. Hamilton engages to deliver up to Col. Clark, Fort Sackville, as it is at present, with all the stores, &c., &c., &c.

2. The garrison are to deliver themselves as prisoners of war, and march out with their arms and accoutrements, &c., &c.

3. The garrison to be delivered up at 10 o'clock to-morrow.

4. Three days' time to be allowed the garrison to settle their accounts with the inhabitants and traders of this place.

5. The officers of the garrison to be allowed the necessary baggage, &c., &c.

Signed at Post St. Vincents, 24th Feb., 1779.

Agreed to for the following reasons: The remoteness from succors; the state and quantity of provisions, &c.; unanimity of officers and men in its expediency; the honourable terms allowed; and, lastly, the confidence in a generous enemy.

(Signed)   HENRY HAMILTON,
Lieut. Gov. and Superintendent.

25th. About 10 o'clock Capt. Bowman and Capt. McCarty's companies paraded on one side of the Fort gate. Governor Hamilton and his garrison marched out, whilst Col. Clark, Captains Williams' and Worthington's companies marched into the Fort, relieved the centries, hoisted the American colours, secured all the arms. Governor Hamilton marched back to the Fort, shut the gate. Orders for thirteen cannon to be fired; during which time there happened a very unlucky accident through mismanagement. There blew up twenty-six six-pound cartridges in one of the batteries, which burned Capt. Bowman and Capt. Worthington much, together with four privates.

No account of our batteau yet.

26th. Rain all day. Captains Helm, Henry, and Major Legare, with fifty men of the militia, ordered to proceed up the river with three boats, with a swivel each, to meet ten boats that were sent in October last, for provisions and stores to Omi, and to take the same in custody.

27th. The *Willing*, our batteau, arrived, to the great mortification of all on board, that they had not the honour to assist us. In the same came William Mires, from Williamsburgh, with very good news. Captain Bowman receives a Major's commission enclosed from the Governor.

28th. Nothing extraordinary.

March *1st.* The officers discharged on parole. Nothing extraordinary.

2d, 3d, and *4th.* Wet weather.

5th. About 10 o'clock Captain Helm arrived. His party took seven boats loaded with provisions and bale-goods, &c., taken from the enemy, with the following prisoners: Mr. Dejean, Grand Judge of Detroit, Mr. Adimar, Commissary, with thirty-eight privates. Letters taken from the enemy, dated Detroit, the 6th February, say, they are much afraid of our people in the spring. Pray Gov. Hamilton to come back again. War was not as yet declared between France and England. Sent off a party of volunteers to Kaskaskias.

6th. A very rainy day. Nothing extraordinary.

7th. Capt. Williams and Lieut. Rogers, with twenty-five men, set off for the Falls of Ohio, to conduct the following prisoners, viz: Lieut. Gov. Hamilton, Major Hays, Capt. Lamoth, Mons. Dejean, Grand Judge of Detroit, Lieut. Shiflin, Doct. M'Beth, Francis M'Ville, Mr. Bell Fenilb, with eighteen privates. Nothing extraordinary.

8th, 9th, 10th, 11th, 13th, and *14th.* Cloudy weather and rain all the foregoing week. This morning Mr. Mires set off for Williamsburg with two men.

15th. A party of Peaians and Meami Indians waited on Col. Clark, and assured him of fidelity, &c., to the Americans, and begged protection. In the meantime there arrived an express from Kaskaskias, by which we learn that Capt. George, with forty-one men, had arrived there from New Orleans, and taken command of Fort Clark; and also that Jas. Willings had resigned his command to the said Capt. George, and that he and Capt. Mackintire had embarked for Philadelphia. Wm. Mires returned, not being able to go by land to the Falls of Ohio, the country overflowing with water.

16*th.* Most of the prisoners took the oath of neutrality, and got permission to set out for Detroit. Sent by them a copy of the alliance between France and the thirteen United States.

17*th.* Nothing extraordinary.

18*th.* Snow and rain the best part of the day.

19*th.* Orders for six boats to be made ready to return to Kaskaskias with prisoners.

20*th.* The boats ready and loaded. Capt. M'Carty takes command of the *Willing;* Capt. Keller, Capt. Worthington, Ensign Montgomery, Ensign Lorraine, each to take charge of one boat. Sergeant and six men to take the small boat called the *Running Fly.* About 4 o'clock the whole embarked, leaving Lieut. Brashers in command of the Fort, with Lieut. Baily, Lieut. Chapman, forty men, Serjeant and Corporals included, to the care of the garrison till relieved from Kaskaskias. Capt. Helm commands the town in all civil matters, and superintendent of Indian affairs, Mr. Moses Henry, Indian Agent, Mr. Patrick Kennedy, Quartermaster. The boats, after rejoicing, are run out of sight. God send them a good and safe passage."

THIS JOURNAL was taken from Major Bowman, and revised by a person who was in the expedition. He has kept it for his own amusement, but it does not come near what might be wrote upon such an extraordinary occasion, had it been handled by a person who chose to enlarge upon it. It afforded matter enough to treat on; the season of the year when undertaken, and the good conduct, shows what might have been done with an army, let the difficulties be what they will. Persevering and steadiness will surmount them all, as was the case with our brave commander, and all his officers, not forgetting his soldiers. Although a handful in comparison to other armies, they have done themselves, and the cause they were fighting for, credit and honour, and deserve a place in history for future ages; that their posterity may know the difficulty their forefathers had gone through for their liberty and freedom. Particularly the back settlers of Virginia may bless the day they sent out such a commander, officers, and men. I say, to root out that nest of vipers, that was every day ravaging on their women and children; which I hope will soon be at an end, as the leaders of these murderers will soon be taken and sent to Congress.

GOD SAVE THE COMMONWEALTH.

Finis.

'79.

(*On the next blank page.*)

GOD SAVE THE COMMONWEALTH, this 15th day of August, 1779.

Index.